# London 2012
# Olympic Games
# The Greatest
# Snow On Earth

First published by Carlton Books Limited 2012

Copyright © 2012 Carlton Books Limited

London 2012 emblems ™ & ® The London Organising Committee of the
Olympic Games and Paralympic Games Ltd (LOCOG) 2007. London 2012
mascots ™ & ® LOCOG 2009-2010. London 2012 pictograms © LOCOG
2009. All Rights Reserved.

Carlton Books Limited,
20 Mortimer Street, London, W1T 3JW

10 9 8 7 6 5 4 3 2 1

ISBN: 978-184732-933-2

Written by The Press Association

Printed in Germany

**Below:** The spectacular sights
of Big Ben and the Houses of
Parliament were two of the iconic
backdrops which epitomised the
London 2012 Olympic Games

# London 2012 Olympic Games

# The Greatest Show On Earth

An official day-by-day photographic celebration

CARLTON

# Contents

# Introduction

**They were the Games that roared. From the Velodrome to the Aquatics Centre to the Olympic Stadium and beyond, the sound of support and appreciation reverberated throughout London 2012**

Britain, the country which gave the world so many of its major sports, put on a show which will live in the memory forever.

It set the tone with a quirky and humorous Opening Ceremony and went on to enthral and entertain for the next 16 days.

With moments of incredible drama coming at such a rapid rate, this book provides a lasting record of the best of the action. Many of the moments will never be forgotten, either by those who were fortunate enough to be present or the millions more watching around the globe, but they are captured here in words and stunning images.

Where do you start when trying to pick out the highlights?

There was Bradley Wiggins, fresh from becoming the first British man to win the Tour de France, taking gold in the Cycling Time Trial amid the splendour of Hampton Court Palace and crowds reminiscent of the Queen's Diamond Jubilee.

In the Olympic Stadium, Jessica Ennis fulfilled her golden destiny in the Heptathlon and the brilliant Mo Farah completed an historic long-distance double.

Felix Sanchez of the Dominican Republic sobbed his heart out on the podium after winning the 400m Hurdles while Kenya's David Rudisha set a stunning world record in the 800m final in a race which pushed the frontiers of the discipline.

In the pool, the USA's Michael Phelps took four golds and twosilvers to overtake Russian Federation gymnast Larissa Latynina as the most decorated Olympian in history with 22 medals, 18 of them gold.

Outside the pool there was a tidal wave of British success, splashing the feel-good factor around an Olympic Park which heaved with packed venues night after night.

The Velodrome rocked to the sound of raucous support as Britain's Jason Kenny and Laura Trott won double gold, Victoria Pendleton won gold and silver before bidding her farewell to the sport in a river of tears, and Chris Hoy surpassed Sir Steve Redgrave as Britain's greatest Olympian with his sixth gold medal.

When it comes to a global superstar though, it is the name of Usain Bolt which will stretch long into the century. Bolt's defence of his 100m title was stupendous in an Olympic record time of 9.63 in the first race in history in which seven of the eight finalists finished in under 10 seconds.

But it was the defence of his 200m title which sealed his legendary status as he became only the second

**Left:** LOCOG Chair Seb Coe declared of the London 2012 Olympic Games, 'We lit the flame and we lit up the world. Once again we have shown ourselves worthy.'

**Opposite:** The passionate support at the Olympic Stadium and across the other Games venues was one of the highlights of London 2012

sprinter in history to retain the two Olympic titles.

What will we remember most? It has to be the sound of patriotic fervour, akin to a force of nature which prevailed on land and sea from Wembley to Weymouth and Portland in two extraordinary weeks.

The Games ran without a hitch and special mention should go to the 70,000 Games Makers who each deserved a medal for their enthusiasm and organisation.

As the curtain came down on London 2012, IOC President Jacques Rogge declared the Games a success, before sharing his hope that the spectacle had fulfilled its brief to 'Inspire a generation'. 'These were happy and glorious Games,' he said. 'The legacy of the Games of the XXX Olympiad will become clear in many ways. The human legacy will reach every region of the world. Many young people will be inspired to take up a sport or to pursue their dreams.'

However, the line of the night belonged to Chair of LOCOG Seb Coe KBE, who proudly declared: 'When our time came Britain, we did it right. Thank you.'

London 2012 truly were the Games that roared.

# Day 0

## London welcomes the Games

The Olympic Games are billed as the greatest show on Earth and it certainly felt that way after a magnificent Opening Ceremony which thrilled those lucky enough to be inside the Olympic Stadium and the millions more watching around the globe.

Celebrating the best of British, it seemed everyone wanted to be involved in the show titled 'Isles of Wonder'.

The Queen made her film debut, boxing legend Muhammad Ali returned to the Olympic stage and David Beckham powered a speedboat up the Thames to deliver the Olympic Torch to its home for the duration of the Games.

The athletes left knowing they had a lot to live up to.

**Right:** A fireworks show begins around the Olympic Stadium as athletes gather around the Cauldron at the climax of the spectacular Opening Ceremony

# Let the Games begin

**As the eyes of the world focused on London, some of the biggest names in sport and entertainment combined to produce an Opening Ceremony which will live long in the memory of all who witnessed it.**

With the official slogan of the London 2012 Games being 'Inspire a generation', it was a fitting gesture to hand the responsibility of lighting the Olympic Cauldron and bringing the curtain down on a blockbusting Opening Ceremony to a group of promising young athletes.

The speculation had been that Sir Roger Bannister, Sir Steve Redgrave or even the Queen herself might light the Cauldron but instead the task was handed to seven unheralded teenagers symbolising the hopes and dreams of Britain's Olympic future.

The youngsters were nominated and accompanied by Great Britain Olympic greats – Lynn Davies, Duncan Goodhew, Dame Kelly Holmes, Dame Mary Peters, Shirley Robertson, Daley Thompson and Sir Steve Redgrave – while it was a more modern British star who got the ball rolling at the start of the night.

Cyclist Bradley Wiggins, who became the first Briton to win the Tour de France less than a week before the start of the Games, rang the bell to begin the Opening Ceremony, which was full of emotion, fun, entertainment, creativity and warmth that sought to remind the world of what makes Britain great.

Cue the rolling meadows and farmyard animals which had been given so much pre-Games publicity. These gave way to grimy chimneys representing the birth of the Industrial Revolution and a nurses' knees-up and lines of hospital beds in honour of the NHS. There was a tribute to those who fell in two world wars, Jerusalem and Shakespeare read by Sir Kenneth Branagh, Peter Pan read by Harry Potter author J.K.Rowling and a pop culture segment with a soundtrack spanning the decades as diverse as the Beatles and the Sex Pistols. *Abide With Me* was spell-binding.

Of course, it was never going to stop at that. Not with Danny Boyle, the film director of *Slumdog Millionaire* fame in charge. There was plenty of humour, not least when 'Mr Bean' was apparently playing keyboard with the London Symphony Orchestra during a rendition of Vangelis's *Chariots of Fire.*

It hit the spot. So, unsurprisingly, did the arrival of the Queen, preceded by a film shot at Buckingham Palace in which she played herself and which ostensibly showed her leaving the Palace in a helicopter with James Bond (actor Daniel Craig), before parachuting into the stadium with 007.

This cut to a shot of the Royal Box and the real Queen, accompanied by the Duke of Edinburgh and Jacques Rogge, President of the International Olympic Committee.

Some time later came the athletes from 204 countries. Usain Bolt led out the Jamaican team, drawing a massive cheer from the crowd. But that was dwarfed by the tickertape reception for Sir Chris Hoy, Britain's flag-bearer, as Team GB became the last nation to enter the Stadium.

Muhammad Ali, his wife attentive, oversaw the raising of the Olympic Flag, before the Queen declared the Games open, just as her father, George VI, had done in 1948.

And as the Cauldron roared into life after a final Torch Relay which included David Beckham bringing it down the River Thames to the Stadium in a speedboat, you could almost feel the spirits soar.

Sir Paul McCartney rounded things off with *Hey Jude* before the now traditional fireworks display ended the night in style.

A cricket match is played in the 'green and pleasant land' section of the Opening Ceremony

**Above:** Tickertape greets Team GB as they are led into the Olympic Stadium by cyclist Sir Chris Hoy

**Left:** Sir Steve Redgrave hands the Olympic Flame to the seven young athletes chosen to light the Cauldron

**Right:** Tour de France winner Bradley Wiggins rings a giant bell to start the Ceremony

**Below:** The Olympic Rings light up with pyrotechnics above the Stadium

**Below right:** The Queen officially declares the London 2012 Games open

The Olympic Stadium pictured from the top of the ArcelorMittal Orbit sculpture, as a dramatic fireworks display lights up the London sky during the Opening Ceremony

# Flying start

**Some athletes were in action before the Games had officially begun and Dong-Hyun Im wasted no time in making his mark at London 2012, while there was plenty of drama in the opening Football matches.**

Hours before the start of the Opening Ceremony, the Games already had its first inspiring and remarkable story of sporting excellence to celebrate.

Lord's Cricket Ground hosted the Archery and a technically blind archer from the Republic of Korea stole the show.

During the men's ranking round, Dong-Hyun Im – whose eyesight is listed at 20/200 – broke his own 72-arrow mark of 696 by three points and was also part of a record in the Team Competition. Alongside Bubmin Kim and Jin Hyek Oh, he helped register a 216-arrow total of 2,087, smashing the world record by 18 points.

The day's Shooting began in perfect conditions, with the Korean trio setting the standard from the off. They took the three top seedings, with world number two Im leading the way and breaking the world record for the third time since the London 2012 test event. Despite rain affecting the second half of the ranking shoot, Im still finished with a superb 699. Kim was just one point behind with 698 and Oh closed with 690. The top four was rounded off by Great Britain's Larry Godfrey, who recorded a personal best of 680.

The host nation did not have as much to cheer in the women's event as Korea again dominated. Naomi Folkard was the highest-ranked British female participant in 42nd place, while six-time Olympian Alison Williamson was 47th.

Great Britain's third Games had started in fine style two days earlier when it fell to the women's Football team to begin the action at the Millennium Stadium in Cardiff. Stephanie Houghton was the Team GB hero on the day as she curled home a superb second-half free-kick to earn a 1-0 win over New Zealand.

In the other match in Group E, Brazil impressed with a 5-0 triumph over Cameroon thanks to a double from captain and five-time world player of the year Marta, while Alex Morgan also scored twice as reigning champions the United States came from 2-0 down to beat France 4-2.

A day later it was the turn of the men to play their first round of group Football matches, which created its fair share of interesting results. Great Britain's hopes of a similar winning start were dashed as Craig Bellamy's first-half goal was not enough to sink Senegal, who grabbed a late equaliser in a 1-1 draw at Old Trafford. More surprisingly, world and European champions Spain fell to a shock defeat in their opening match as Japan claimed a 1-0 win with a hugely impressive performance at Hampden Park.

Belarus marked their first appearance at a major tournament since gaining independence 21 years earlier with a 1-0 win over New Zealand, while pre-tournament favourites Brazil survived a fightback from Egypt to triumph 3-2.

Korean archer Dong-Hyun Im collects his arrows after setting a new world record

'**The girls have made history. We couldn't ignore it. We were the first women's GB team ever and we won. That will never change now**'

*Team GB women's Football manager Hope Powell*

# For the record

## World records
### Archery – men's Individual
Dong-Hyun Im (Republic of Korea) 699

### Archery – men's Team
Republic of Korea (Dong-Hyun Im, Bubmin Kim, Jin Hyek Oh) 2,087

**Above left:** Japan's Yuki Otsu celebrates the goal that gave his side a shock win over Spain at Hampden Park

**Left:** Brazil's women's Football superstar Marta started ominously with two goals in the 5-0 win over Cameroon

**Above:** Craig Bellamy was in the thick of the action and gave the Great Britain men's team the lead against Senegal

**Below:** The scene on the first day of the Games as Archery took over the home of cricket at Lord's before the Opening Ceremony

# Day 1

## Saturday, 28 July 2012

## Going for gold

**Archery**
Men's Team Competition

**Cycling**
Men's Road Race

**Fencing**
Women's Individual Foil

**Judo**
Women's Extra Lightweight (up to 48kg)
• Men's Extra Lightweight (up to 60kg)

**Shooting**
Women's 10m Air Rifle • Men's 10m
Air Pistol

**Swimming**
Men's 400m Individual Medley • Men's
400m Freestyle • Women's 400m Individual
Medley • Women's 4 x 100m Freestyle Relay

**Weightlifting**
Women's 48kg

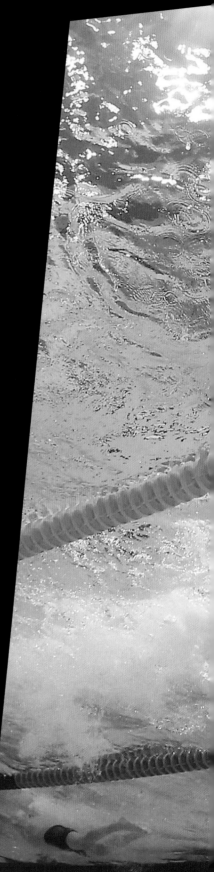

**Right:** United States swimmer Ryan Lochte
on his way to victory in the men's 400m
Individual Medley, stealing the thunder of
compatriot Michael Phelps, the multiple
Olympic champion who could only finish
fourth in the final

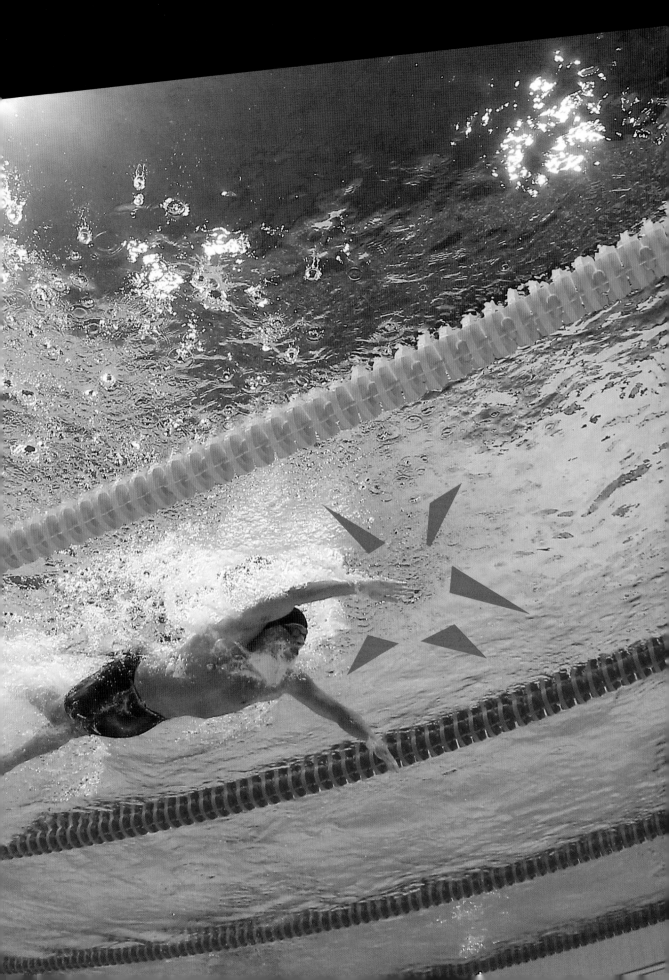

# Gold run begins

**The first medals of the London 2012 Games were handed out to deserving champions as iconic London landmarks and stunning new venues all witnessed sporting drama on the first full day of action.**

The return of Michael Phelps to an Olympic Games swimming pool for the first time since clinching his record eighth gold medal at Beijing 2008 was billed as the must-see attraction on the first full day of action at London 2012.

There was one man who clearly had not read the script though, as United States team-mate Ryan Lochte emerged from the shadows of his great rival to take gold in the 400m Individual Medley in fine style. The manner of his victory – by a margin of more than three-and-a-half seconds – was not wholly unexpected as he had won the world title in 2011 on his way to five gold medals. It was the sight of Phelps trailing home in

fourth, behind silver medallist Thiago Pereira of Brazil and Japanese 17-year-old Kosuke Hagino in third, which surprised the most.

The legendary swimmer came into the Games knowing three medals would place him as the most successful Olympian of all time. But in the first of his seven events, Phelps only squeezed into the final of the 400m Individual Medley race as the eighth fastest during the morning heats and found himself in lane eight for the evening medal showdown, where he stood third at the halfway stage before dropping out of contention on the breaststroke leg.

It was a night of drama as the first medals were handed out

at the Aquatics Centre, with Australia winning gold ahead of the Netherlands and the USA in a very tight women's 4 x 100m Freestyle Relay final.

But Day 2 very much belonged to China, both in and out of the pool. Looking to make a good start in their quest to beat their gold medal tally of 51 from Beijing 2008, the Chinese team picked up four titles.

Shooter Siling Yi got the ball rolling by becoming the first gold medal winner of the Games in the women's 10m Air Rifle, before four-time world champion Mingjuan Wang secured the women's 48kg Weightlifting title.

Better was to come for China in the Swimming, however, as Yang Sun became the first male swimmer from his country to win gold in the sport with his victory in the men's 400m Freestyle final in a new Olympic record, before Shiwen Ye produced a magnificent freestyle leg in the final of the women's 400m Individual Medley to set a new world record at only 16.

Another nation with much to celebrate was Italy, who enjoyed a clean sweep in the women's Individual Foil Fencing competition. Elisa Di Francisca took gold after beating Arianna Errigo 12-11 in a final that went to sudden death.

Shooter Siling Yi wipes away a tear after winning the first gold medal of the Games

**' There is no better way than to start than with an Olympic gold. Having the family here cheering for me definitely gave me a boost '**

*United States gold medallist Ryan Lochte*

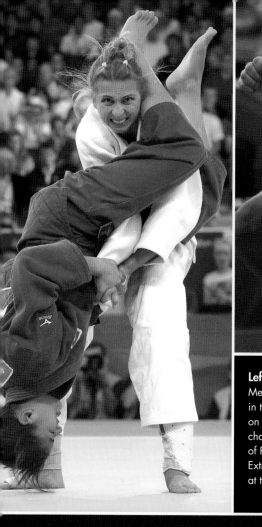

**Left:** Brazil's Sarah Menezes (in blue) looks in trouble but goes on to beat defending champion Alina Dumitru of Romania in the Judo Extra Lightweight (-48kg) at the ExCeL

**Above:** Michele Frangilli is congratulated after he hit a maximum 10 with his final arrow to win the men's Archery Team Competition final for Italy against the USA at Lord's Cricket Ground

**Below:** Elisa Di Francisca scores the all-important winning hit to beat her Italian team-mate Arianna Errigo and take the gold medal in the women's Fencing Individual Foil event

The pre-tournament favourite had been 38-year-old Valentina Vezzali, who was bidding for an historic fourth consecutive gold medal, but she had to settle for bronze in even more dramatic fashion.

Vezzali, who had carried Italy's flag at the Opening Ceremony the night before, came back from the huge disappointment of losing her semi-final to team-mate Errigo to beat Nam Hyun-hee, the Korean she beat in the Beijing 2008 final, in overtime. The police officer trailed Nam 12-8 with only 13 seconds remaining, but levelled with a second to go and then triumphed.

## The perfect 10

That success for Italy came hours after a nailbiting affair in the Archery at Lord's Cricket Ground, where Michele Frangilli showed nerves of steel to hit a 10 with the last arrow of the men's Team final to clinch a 219-218 victory over the United States.

A total of 12 gold medals were handed out on the day across seven different sports. Two of them were in Judo as Brazil's Sarah Menezes beat defending champion Alina Dumitru of Romania in the women's Judo Extra Lightweight (-48kg) category. Russian Arsen Galstyan produced another shock in the men's Extra Lightweight (-60kg) event as he defeated double world champion Rishod Sobirov of Uzbekistan on a 'golden score' in additional time after their semi-final ended level, before overcoming Japan's Hiroaki Hiraoka in the final with a superb ippon throw after only 40 seconds.

Elsewhere, Republic of Korea shooter Jin Jong Oh won the men's 10m Air Pistol, while Kazakhstan's

Alexandr Vinokourov was the surprise winner of the men's Cycling Road Race, which finished on The Mall.

In the build-up to the Games, there were high expectations that world champion Mark Cavendish would give the host nation the perfect start to London 2012 by winning their first gold medal but despite having Tour de France winner Bradley Wiggins and runner-up Chris Froome helping him, the rest of the field were not ready to hand victory on a plate to the Isle of Man star. A series of breakaways during the 250-kilometre event made life hard for the British team and despite riding hard at the front of the peloton, they were unable to claw back the gap to the leaders. It was left to 38-year-old Vinokourov to see off Colombia's Rigoberto Uran in a sprint to the line to go one better than the silver he won at Sydney 2000 and complete his comeback following a broken leg suffered during the 2011 Tour de France.

Hannah Miley had been the other big Team GB medal hope but could only manage fifth in the 400m Individual Medley race won by Chinese teenager Ye. But it was not all doom and gloom for the hosts, who had much to feel encouraged about in the Artistic Gymnastics. In the men's qualification round, the squad of Louis Smith, Daniel Purvis, Kristian Thomas, Max Whitlock and Sam Oldham saw off reigning champions China to lead Great Britain to their first Olympic Games men's Team Competition final in 88 years.

In the Rowing, three British crews won their heats, including Helen Glover and Heather Stanning in the women's Pair, who set a new Olympic record to book their place in the final and confirm their status as favourites.

Even more impressive was the performance of New Zealand duo Hamish Bond and Eric Murray, who destroyed the world's best time set by Matthew Pinsent and James Cracknell at the 2002 World Championships.

The men's Cycling Road Race reached its climax on The Mall in front of Buckingham Palace

' **It's been an emotional four years for the whole of British gymnastics. There's been a lot of pressure since Beijing to perform at these Olympics** '

*Team GB gymnast Louis Smith*

**Above:** Kristian Thomas on the parallel bars during a fine opening day in the Gymnastics for Team GB's men

**Left:** Full-back Stephanie Houghton scores for the second successive game as Great Britain beat Cameroon 3-0 in the women's Football

**Right:** The dramatic scene as the sun sets over the Beach Volleyball at Horse Guards Parade

**Left:** Mingjuan Wang wins the women's -48kg Weightlifting for China

# For the record

## World records

**Rowing – men's Pair**
Eric Murray and Hamish Bond (New Zealand) 6:08.50

**Swimming – women's 400m Individual Medley**
Ye Shiwen (China) 4:28.43

## Olympic records

**Rowing – women's pair**
Helen Glover and Heather Stanning (Great Britain) 6:57.29

**Rowing – men's Double Sculls**
Nathan Cohen and Joseph Sullivan (New Zealand) 6:11.30

**Rowing – men's Single Sculls**
Tim Maeyens (Belgium) 6:42.52

**Swimming – men's 400m Freestyle**
Sun Yang (China) 3:40.14

**Swimming – men's 100m Breaststroke**
Cameron van der Burgh (South Africa) 58.83

**Swimming – women's 100m Butterfly**
Dana Vollmer (USA) 56.25

**Swimming – women's 4 x 100m Freestyle Relay**
Australia (Alicia Coutts, Cate Campbell, Brittany Elmslie
and Melanie Schlange) 03:33.15

## Team GB moment of the day

Anthony Ogogo could have been forgiven for treating London 2012 as an irrelevant sideshow given his family turmoil in the build-up.

Ogogo's mother Teresa was taken seriously ill six weeks before the start of the Games after suffering a brain haemorrhage, but the British boxer showed great bravery to turn out on the first full day of action and won his first-round fight in convincing fashion at ExCeL.

Ogogo said his mother's fight inspired him to produce a strong and focused performance against his opponent from the Dominican Republic, Junior Castillo, as he eased away to score a 13-6 victory and earn a place in the last 16 of the Middleweight competition. After his win, he then made a flying visit back to his native Norfolk that evening to visit his mother.

## Golden Games moment

After their world-record feats in the Archery ranking round, Korea's men looked nailed on for gold at Lord's Cricket Ground.

But in a dramatic competition, the Koreans lost to the United States in the semi-finals as world number one Brady Ellison helped book a place in the final against the Italians. It was then the turn of the USA to fall to the underdogs as Italy claimed a shock gold thanks to star archer Michele Frangilli.

Italy, who had never before won team gold at the Games, were nine behind with one shot remaining and, despite being under massive pressure to deliver, Frangilli held his nerve to hit a 10 with the last arrow of the final for a 219-218 win. Frangilli's heroics saw him complete a full set of medals in the Team Competition event, having picked up bronze at Atlanta in 1996 and silver at Sydney four years later. ∎

# Day 2

## Sunday, 29 July 2012

## Going for gold

**Archery**
Women's Team Competition

**Cycling**
Women's Road Race

**Diving**
Women's Synchronised 3m Springboard

**Fencing**
Men's Individual Sabre

**Judo**
Women's Half-Lightweight (48-52kg)
• Men's Half-Lightweight (60-66kg)

**Shooting**
Women's 10m Air Pistol • Women's Skeet

**Swimming**
Women's 100m Butterfly • Men's 100m Breaststroke •
Women's 400m Freestyle • Men's 4 x 100m Freestyle Relay

**Weightlifting**
Men's 56kg • Women's 53kg

**Right:** Marianne Vos of the Netherlands
celebrates her victory in the women's
Cycling Road Race in pouring rain on The
Mall, just pipping Great Britain's Lizzie
Armitstead, whose silver was the host
nation's first medal of London 2012

# Drama and delight

**The home crowds had plenty to cheer about as Great Britain's Lizzie Armitstead and Rebecca Adlington won the host nation's first medals with impressive performances in the Cycling and Swimming.**

Day 2 of the London 2012 Olympic Games was greeted by thunder and grey skies, but cyclist Lizzie Armitstead ensured every cloud had a silver lining for Great Britain as she secured the host nation's first medal by finishing second in the women's Road Race.

Armitstead was beaten to victory by the Netherlands' Marianne Vos at the end of a pulsating 140km race, which featured two climbs of Surrey's Box Hill. After breaking away from the peloton along with Vos and eventual bronze medallist Olga Zabelinskaya, the 23-year-old looked odds-on to claim Great Britain's first podium success of the Games, but the colour was yet to be decided. Armitstead positioned herself behind the Dutchwoman as they cycled on

to The Mall in the closing stages, but Vos was strong enough to hold off the Briton, who had to settle for second.

Team GB will have hoped the result could prove to be a good omen for the remainder of the Games, having won their first medal at Beijing 2008 on a rainy day in the same event, when Nicole Cooke was crowned champion.

Later, on another busy night at the Aquatics Centre, Rebecca Adlington made her own contribution to the early British medal tally, putting in a performance filled with her customary guts and determination to finish an unexpected third in the women's 400m Freestyle. Despite being the reigning Olympic champion, the 23-year-old had only scraped into the final earlier in the

day and was forced to swim out in lane eight against a strong field.

The result was made even more remarkable by the fact Adlington recorded a faster time to claim bronze than she had to win gold four years earlier, with the race being won by France's Camille Muffat in a new Olympic record of 4:01.45, with American Allison Schmitt second.

The first gold medal of the night in the pool went to Dana Vollmer of the United States, who cruised to victory in the women's 100m Butterfly, breaking the world record in the process with a time of 55.93. She had been favourite coming in to the final, having set an Olympic record in her heat, and took 0.08 seconds off Sarah Sjostrom's 2009 world best time in what was another

Dana Vollmer of the United States set a new world record in the women's 100m Butterfly

**❝ Once I got out it was unbelievable. That's what being on home soil is all about, no matter where you come the crowd has that reaction ❞**

*Rebecca Adlington on winning bronze for Great Britain in the women's 400m Freestyle*

**Above:** Camille Muffat shows her delight after winning the women's 400m Freestyle in an Olympic record time. Great Britain's Rebecca Adlington (below) took bronze

**Right:** Daniel Sturridge scores a brilliant third goal to cap Great Britain's 3-1 win over the United Arab Emirates in the men's Football at Wembley Stadium

Yun Chol Om emerged from the B group to win the 56kg Weightlifting Olympic title

commanding performance from the New York-born star. South Africa's Cameron van der Burgh was another swimmer to break a world record as he won the men's100m Breaststroke in 58.46, leaving Australia's Christian Sprenger in second and the USA's Brendan Hansen third.

Despite picking up the 17th Olympic Games medal of his career, it was another night of disappointment for Michael Phelps, whose contribution was not enough as his USA quartet – who had led the 4 x 100m Relay final almost throughout – allowed the French team to pass them in the final 50m to snatch gold and claim the country's second gold of the evening.

Earlier on at the Aquatics Centre, China's Minxia Wu secured her place in Games history by winning her third consecutive Synchronised 3m Springboard title, alongside Zi He, at the opening diving event of London 2012. Another athlete writing herself into the Games history books was USA shooter Kimberly Rhode, who won gold in the women's Skeet. The 33-year-old, who had set a new Olympic record in qualifying with 74 hits out of 75, equalled her own world record with a perfect 25 in

the final for a total of 99 in front of a packed shotgun range at The Royal Artillery Barracks. The result made Rhode the first American to win an individual medal at five consecutive Olympic Games, having won gold in the Double Trap event in 1996 and 2004, a bronze in 2000, and bagging silver in the Skeet at Beijing four years ago.

In the women's 10m Air Pistol, Wenjun Guo built on China's strong start to the Games to win her country's second Shooting gold medal in dramatic fashion. Celine Goberville of France looked on course to spring a surprise and dethrone the reigning champion as she led going into the final shot, but her last effort was wayward, scoring a lowly 8.8, leaving Guo to nail a near-perfect 10.8 to retain her title.

## Weighty subject
One of the day's major stories came at ExCeL, where Yun Chol Om of DPR Korea claimed Weightlifting gold in sensational style, after double world champion and pre-competition favourite Jingbiao Wu failed to make his last lift in a thrilling finale to the 56kg category. Amazingly, Om triumphed from the morning's

B group – supposedly for second-tier lifters – and set a new Olympic record in the clean & jerk element, lifting 168kg. Kazakhstan's Zulfiya Chinshanlo won gold in the women's 53 kg, lifting 131kg to set a new Olympic Games and world record, contributing to a total 226kg – another Olympic record.

The Republic of Korea continued their impressive Archery record with a 210-209 victory over China in the final of the women's Team Competition, their seventh consecutive title in the event. The match was decided on the last arrow, when Bo Bae Ki needed at least nine to secure victory and duly hit the outer gold to prompt wild celebrations with her team-mates.

In the Fencing, Aron Szilagyi continued his country's proud tradition in the men's Individual Sabre as he claimed Hungary's 13th Olympic Games title in the event. The 22-year-old was the nation's only representative in the 36-strong field, but after four earlier wins he beat Italian Diego Occhiuzzi 15-8 in the final to become the youngest gold medal winner in the event since Greece's Ioannis Georgiadis won at Athens 1896. The Judo finals saw Georgia's Lashas Shavdatuashvili win the men's Half-Lightweight category, while Kum Ae An of DPR Korea was crowned champion in the equivalent women's competition.

The Great Britain men's football team ended Day 2 by securing a 3-1 victory over the United Arab Emirates – the first Olympic Games win for the team since 1960 – with goals coming from Ryan Giggs, Scott Sinclair and Daniel Sturridge. More joy came for the host nation at the Artistic Gymnastics, where a magnificent performance from Beth Tweddle on the Uneven Bars during the qualification round inspired Team GB into the final of the women's Team Competition.

Minxia Wu won
a third successive
Synchronised 3m
Springboard gold
medal, alongside
Chinese partner
Zi He

# For the record

## World records

**Swimming – men's 100m Breaststroke**
Cameron van der Burgh (South Africa) 58.46

**Swimming – women's 100m Butterfly**
Dana Vollmer (USA) 55.98

**Weightlifting – women's 53kg**
Zulfiya Chinshanlo (Kazakhstan) 226kg

## Olympic records

**Shooting – women's Skeet**
Kimberley Rhode (USA) 99

**Swimming – women's 100m Backstroke**
Emily Seebohm (Australia) 58.23

**Swimming – women's 400m Freestyle**
Camille Muffat (France) 4:01.45

**Weightlifting – men's 56kg**

**Above left:** Germany's Hannes Aigner competes in the men's Canoe Slalom Kayak (K1) under dark skies at the Lee Valley White Water Centre

**Far left:** Bo Bae Ki needed at least nine with the final arrow to win the women's Archery Team final for the Republic of Korea – and did it

**Left:** Zulfiya Chinshanlo of Kazakhstan, who set a new world record of 131kg in the clean and jerk element of the women's 53kg Weightlifting

**Above:** Beth Tweddle registered the highest score on the Uneven Bars as Great Britain qualified for the final of the women's Gymnastics Team event

**Below:** Kimberley Rhode of the United States earned a medal for the fifth successive Games as she won the Skeet in the women's Shooting

## Team GB moment of the day

Four years earlier at Beijing 2008, Great Britain's first medal came during a rainy women's Cycling Road Race when Nicole Cooke claimed gold. On a wet and thundery Sunday in London, Lizzie Armitstead set out to continue that trend, and took the silver medal behind the Netherlands' Marianne Vos. After making a break from the peloton along with Vos and Olga Zabelinskaya, Armitstead's sprint finish was not quite enough to beat her Dutch counterpart, but earned herself the honour of securing her country's first appearance on the podium at London 2012.

## Golden Games moment

In Weightlifting, DPR Korea's Yun Chol Om caused a sensation in the men's 56kg division when he equalled the world's best clean & jerk of 168kg to set a new Olympic record and, in the process, became only the fifth man in history to lift triple his own body weight. Om's marker would not be matched by any athlete in the A group after

# Day 3

Monday, 30 July 2012

## Going for gold

**Diving**
Men's Synchronised 10m Platform

**Fencing**
Women's Individual Epée

**Gymnastics**
Men's Team Competition

**Judo**
Women's Lightweight • Men's Lightweight

**Shooting**
Men's 10m Air Rifle

**Swimming**
Men's 200m Freestyle • Women's 100m Backstroke •
Men's 100m Backstroke • Women's 100m Breaststroke

**Weightlifting**
Women's 58kg • Men's 62kg

**Right:** Louis Smith in action on the
pommel horse as Great Britain earned

# Magical Monday

**Success for Great Britain's gymnasts and a Lithuanian teenager in the pool were the unexpected highlights of another thrilling day in London as China's gold medal collection continued to grow.**

The first Monday of the London 2012 Olympic Games proved to be a historic one for Great Britain's gymnasts, who turned in a sensational performance to secure the country's first medal in the men's Team Competition for a century.

The bronze medal-winning team, consisting of Louis Smith, Max Whitlock, Daniel Purvis, Sam Oldham and Kristian Thomas, had initially been awarded second place, sparking raucous celebrations at the North Greenwich Arena, where spectators included the Duke of Cambridge and Prince Harry. An inquiry into the score of Kohei Uchimura's pommel horse routine then saw Japan jump from fourth to second and Britain downgraded to bronze, but it could not take the shine off a stunning achievement.

The British team, who had caused a surprise by qualifying third for the final, were in or around the medal positions throughout. There were concerns for their podium prospects late on when Oldham fell from the horizontal bar – Team GB's penultimate apparatus – but the team pulled through to finish ahead of their close rivals Ukraine.

China's final score of 275.997 meant they successfully defended their Olympic title, while 2008 silver medallists Japan leapfrogged Britain's score of 271.711, with an upgraded total of 271.952 to again secure second spot. Ukraine faced the biggest heartbreak as they were denied a bronze medal by the Japanese appeal.

Members of the Royal Family had earlier been at Greenwich Park to watch Zara Phillips, the Queen's granddaughter, produce a commanding performance on her Olympic debut as Great Britain's eventers kept their gold medal dream alive. They ended the day in second place behind reigning European champions Germany, who were on a score of 124.70, 5.5 penalties ahead of Britain, with Sweden third.

The Aquatics Centre was the location for one of the day's most highly-anticipated events as London 2012 poster boy Tom Daley lined up with diving partner Peter Waterfield in the men's Synchronised 10m Platform. They led the competition at the halfway mark and were roared on by a vocal home support but they faded thereafter. A pair of errors,

Great Britain's men's Gymnastics team celebrating a first medal for a century

**' We're a team. At the end of the day that's it, full stop. We're a team and we win together and we lose together '**

*Disappointed Great Britain diver Tom Daley*

**Above:** Zara Phillips, the Queen's granddaughter, in action during the cross-country phase of the Eventing Team Competition at Greenwich Park

**Right:** Peter Waterfield and Tom Daley of Great Britain perform in the men's Synchronised 10m Platform

**Bottom:** The scene at the Riverbank Arena as Great Britain's men's Hockey team beat Argentina 4-1

most notably on their reverse three-and-a-half somersaults dive, cost them dear and Chinese teenagers and competition favourites Yuan Cao and Yanquan Zhang claimed gold. Mexico and the United States took silver and bronze respectively, leaving the British pair in fourth, agonisingly close to a podium finish.

There was a shock in the pool later in the evening as 15-year-old Ruta Meilutyte won Lithuania's first ever Swimming gold in the women's 100m Breaststroke. Meilutyte, who trains in Plymouth and attends the same school as Daley, successfully fended off a field that included reigning Olympic champion Leisel Jones and Rebecca Soni, who won silver in the event for the second consecutive Games.

After winning two gold medals in the pool on Day 2, the Aquatics Centre once again proved to be a happy hunting ground for French swimmers as Yannick Agnel added to his 4 x 100m Freestyle Relay gold by winning the men's 200m Freestyle. The 20-year-old stormed into an early lead and never looked back – touching the wall almost two seconds ahead of Taehwan Park, who claimed silver.

The United States also enjoyed a successful evening in the water, Missy Franklin taking the first of their gold medals in the women's 100m Backstroke, finishing ahead of Australia's Emily Seebohm, who had set a new Olympic record the previous day. Matthew Grevers doubled the country's gold medal haul for the evening with victory in the men's 100m Backstroke, setting a new Olympic record time of 52.16 on his way to glory.

Over at London's ExCeL, Un Guk Kim claimed Weightlifting gold in style for the Democratic People's Republic of Korea in an exciting men's 62kg competition which saw Olympic and world records tumble. Kim followed up a snatch of 153kg, which broke the Olympic record and equalled the world best, with a clean & jerk of 174kg, providing him with an impressive personal best total of 327kg, which also smashed both records. The Olympic record for clean & jerk also fell as Oscar Albeiro Figueroa Mosquera lifted 177kg to help rack up a total of 317kg as he claimed silver. China's Xueying Li claimed gold in the women's 58kg, setting a new Games record in the snatch (108kg) and total (246kg), while equalling the clean & jerk best (138kg).

Japan's Kaori Matsumoto won gold by beating Romania's Corina Caprioriu in dramatic fashion in the women's Lightweight Judo. The Romanian was disqualified during the extra time 'golden score' period of the final for trying to hold Matsumoto's leg to flip her over. Japan went close to claiming a second Judo gold of the day when Riki Nakaya reached the final of the men's Lightweight competition, but the 23-year-old was beaten by Mansur Isaev of Russia.

Yana Shemyakina won Ukraine's first individual Fencing gold in the Individual Epée when she beat Germany's 2008 champion Britta Heidemann in a final that went into a minute's extra time when they tied 8-8. The Ukrainian achieved the decisive hit as the bout headed into the last 30 seconds.

## Shooting stars

The Royal Artillery Barracks provided the setting for a tight battle between Romanian shooter Alin George Moldoveanu and world number one Niccolo Campriani of Italy in the final of the men's 10m Air Rifle. The duo had both topped the qualification by equalling the Olympic record and swapped top spots in the final a number of times before Moldoveanu emerged with the gold medal. The Romanian held his nerve with a final shot of 10.3 to hold off his rival, who finished a mere 0.6 points behind.

There were no medals on offer at Eton Dorney on Day 3, but that did not stop some rowers putting in record-breaking performances. Great Britain's Katherine Grainger and Anna Watkins underlined their status as gold medal favourites in the women's Double Sculls by setting a new Olympic best time in qualifying for the final. The double world champions destroyed the previous Games best – set by Germany in Barcelona 20 years earlier – by nearly five seconds as they won their heat in 6:44.33. Australia's men's Four team made their own contribution to a superb morning on the water by setting an Olympic record time of 5:47.06, securing their place in the competition's semi-finals.

Great Britain's Katherine Grainger and Anna Watkins set a new Olympic record in the heats of the women's Double Sculls

London 2012

Un Guk Kim of DPR Korea shows his delight as he wins the men's Weightlifting 62kg competition with a new world and Olympic record total of 327kg

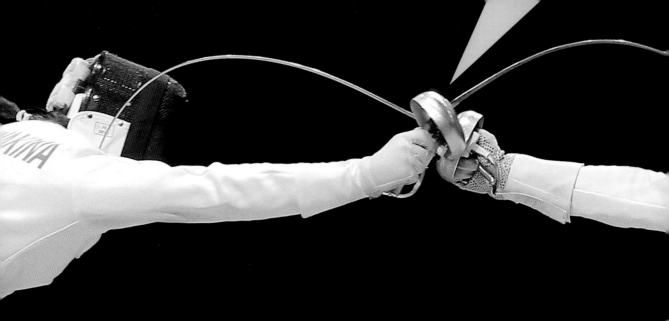

**Above:** Yana Shemyakina of Ukraine (left) and Germany's Britta Heidemann lunging simultaneously in the final of the women's Individual Epée. Shemyakina won gold in extra time

**Right:** Alin George Moldoveanu of Romania (on the left) won the men's 10m Air Rifle by a margin of only 0.6 points at The Royal Artillery Barracks

**Far right:** 15-year-old Ruta Meilutyte, who trains in Plymouth, celebrating Lithuania's first ever Swimming gold medal in the women's 100m Breaststroke

**Below:** United States Tennis star Andy Roddick in action during his win over Martin Klizan of Slovakia in the first round of the men's Singles

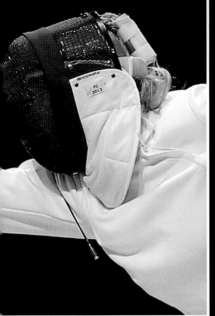

# For the record

## World records
**Weightlifting – men's 62kg**
Un Guk Kim (DPR Korea) 327kg

## Olympic records

**Rowing – women's Double Sculls**
Katherine Grainger and Anna Watkins (Great Britain) 6:44.33

**Rowing – men's Four**
Australia 5:47.06

**Swimming – men's 100m Backstroke**
Matthew Grevers (USA) 52.16

**Swimming – women's 200m Individual Medley**
Shiwen Ye (China) 2:08.39

**Weightlifting – women's 58kg**
Xueying Li (China) 246kg

## Team GB moment of the day

Great Britain's gymnasts had not won a medal in the men's Team Competition
for 100 years and took a lot of people by surprise when they qualified
third for the final. Not only had they not won a medal for a century, but
Great Britain had not competed in the discipline since Barcelona hosted
the Olympic Games in 1992.

The team, consisting of Louis Smith, Max Whitlock, Daniel Purvis, Sam
Oldham and Kristian Thomas, defied history to sensationally win a bronze
medal and it could have been even better had it not been for a successful
appeal from Japan, who protested the Pommel Horse score of one of
their gymnasts. The inquiry resulted in Japan leapfrogging Team GB in
to second place, but the outcome did not dampen the home crowd's spirits
in the North Greenwich Arena.

## Golden Games moment

For most 15-year-old girls, July is a time for going on holiday with family
or meeting up with friends and enjoying a well-earned break from school.
That was not the case for Lithuanian swimmer Ruta Meilutyte, who marked
her summer holidays by winning her country's first ever Olympic gold
medal in the pool.

In a field that included reigning Olympic champion Leisel Jones and
2008 silver medallist Rebecca Soni, Meilutyte stormed to glory in the 100m
Breaststroke. The final had been delayed by a few minutes but any thoughts
that it may have added to any nerves the youngster was suffering from were
soon dispelled. She made a flying start to lead from start to finish and touched
in 1:05.47 as she held off the fast-finishing Soni. ∎

# Day 4

## Going for gold

**Canoe Slalom**
Men's Canoe Single (C1)

**Diving**
Women's Synchronised 10m Platform

**Equestrian**
Eventing Team Competition • Eventing Individual
Competition

**Fencing**
Men's Individual Foil

**Gymnastics**
Women's Team Competition

**Judo**
Women's Half-Middleweight (57-63kg)
• Men's Half-Middleweight (73-81kg)

**Shooting**
Men's Skeet

**Swimming**
Women's 200m Freestyle • Men's 200m Butterfly •
Women's 200m Individual Medley • Men's 4 x 200m
Freestyle Relay

**Weightlifting**
Women's 63kg • Men's 69kg

**Right:** Swimmer Michael Phelps became
the greatest Olympian of all time in terms
of medals won when he anchored the
United States quartet to victory in the men's
4 x 200m Freestyle Relay to win his 19th medal

# History is made

**United States swimmer Michael Phelps became the most successful Olympian of all time when he won his 19th medal, including his 15th gold, on a day of momentous achievements in a number of sports at the Games.**

Day 4 of London 2012 saw Michael Phelps swim into the history books as he reached the phenomenal feat of becoming the most decorated Olympian of all time.

Phelps' final leg in the 4 x 200m Freestyle Relay secured gold for the United States team and took the Baltimore swimmer to a staggering total of 19 career Olympic Games medals, surpassing the previous record of 18 held by the Soviet Union's Larissa Latynina – who dominated women's Gymnastics between 1956 and 1964. However, Phelps did not have things all his own way in the Aquatics Centre and was narrowly beaten to the men's 200m Butterfly gold by South Africa's Chad le Clos. Having led the race throughout, Phelps was overtaken by le Clos at the last possible moment, missing out on the gold medal by only 0.05 seconds.

Phelps was not the only US swimmer with something to shout about on the first Tuesday of the Games, as Allison Schmitt dominated the women's 200m Freestyle from start to finish to win gold in a new Olympic record time of 1:53.61, fending off competition from Camille Muffat of France and Australia's Bronte Barratt. There was also another gold medal for China's Shiwen Ye, who triumphed in the women's 200m Individual Medley – her second victory at London 2012.

At Greenwich Park's Equestrian arena, Germany's Michael Jung had a 30th birthday to remember as he galloped to gold aboard his horse Sam to become the first ever competitor to simultaneously hold the

Michael Phelps shows off his 19th Olympic medal and 15th gold

world, European and Olympic titles in Eventing's Individual Competition. The victory followed his involvement in the Team success for the Germans, who fought off the challenge of a strong British quintet who had entered the final day in second place. The team, consisting of William Fox-Pitt, Zara Phillips, Mary King, Tina Cook and Nicola Wilson, managed to hold on to their position to claim a silver medal, with Cook's jumping round, which included just one time fault, securing the result. The podium finish meant Phillips, the Queen's granddaughter, became the first member of the British royal family to win an Olympic medal and saw her emulate her father, Captain Mark Phillips, who won a medal at the Games 40 years earlier by taking gold in Munich. The Victory Ceremony was also a real family affair as the Princess Royal presented her daughter with the silver medal. However, the Brits could not transfer their Team Competition success to the Individual Competition and, despite looking well-placed to secure a medal, King and Cook both had four faults to finish outside the medals, while Phillips was eighth.

There was a shock result at the North Greenwich Arena, where

> ❝ I told those guys (4 x 200m Freestyle Relay team-mates) I wanted a big lead in the last leg and they gave it to me. I just wanted to hold on ❞

*United States swimmer Michael Phelps on winning medal number 19 at the Olympic Games*

**Above:** Zara Phillips (far left) and her Great Britain colleagues won the silver medal in the Eventing Team Competition

**Right:** Gabrielle Douglas' floor routine helped the United States take gold in the women's Gymnastics Team Competition

**Below:** Shiwen Ye of China won her second gold of the Games in the women's 200m Individual Medley

**Below right:** US Army Sergeant Vincent Hancock retained his men's Skeet title – the first person to do so in Games history – with a new Olympic record score of 148 points

the United States claimed gold in the women's Artistic Gymnastics Team Competition ahead of Russia and Romania, who took silver and bronze respectively, while reigning champions China were left distraught as they missed out on a place on the podium. Britain's women failed to repeat the achievements of their male counterparts, who won bronze in the men's event the day before, but their sixth-place finish delivered Team GB's best women's Gymnastics Team Competition result since the Amsterdam 1928 Games.

Two of Canoe Slalom's most decorated competitors went head-to-head in the Canoe Single (C1) Competition at Lee Valley White Water Centre. Tony Estanguet and Michal Martikan were both in contention for medals, but it was Frenchman Estanguet who claimed gold. The victory added to the titles he won at Sydney 2000 and Athens 2004 but the 34-year-old had not been expected to triumph again. He received his gold medal in torrential rain in front of thousands of spectators, who had stayed in the stands to cheer him. Slovakia's Martikan was forced to settle for bronze, notching his fifth Olympic medal, having previously won two golds and two silvers, while Germany's Sideris Tasiadis took silver.

US Army Sergeant Vincent Hancock had cause for celebration at the Royal Artillery Barracks as he became the first Skeet shooter to retain an Olympic title – doing so in record-breaking fashion. The 23-year-old from Columbus, Georgia, broke his own Olympic record, missing just two shots and firing a perfect 25 in the final to register a total of 148 points. Hancock finished two points ahead of Denmark's Anders Golding, who claimed silver, while Nasser Al-Attiya of Qatar, who is a regular competitor in the Dakar Rally and won the prestigious motor event in 2011, took bronze after a shoot-off with Russia's Valeriy Shomin.

At London's ExCeL, Maiya Maneza won the women's 63kg Weightlifting with a record-breaking performance to claim Kazakhstan's third gold of the Games. Maneza took victory with her first clean & jerk attempt at 135kg – equalling the Olympic record – before breaking another with her total of 245kg. In the men's 69kg division, Qingfeng Lin comprehensively took the field apart lifting a total of 344kg, with silver going to Indonesia's Triyatno and Romania's 20-year-old Razvan Constantin Martin clinching bronze.

China's Sheng Lei took gold in the men's Individual Foil, while 21-year-old Egyptian Alaaeldin Abouelkassem made history by winning silver, Africa's first-ever Olympic Games Fencing medal. There were two gold medals on offer in the Judo, where Jae-Bum Kim of the Republic of Korea and Slovenia's Urska Zolnir emerged victorious in the men's Half-Middleweight (73-81kg) and women's Half-Middleweight (57-63kg) finals respectively.

## China's hat-trick

Ruolin Chen and Hao Wang of China lived up to expectations as they cruised to a comfortable victory in the women's Synchronised 10m Platform, claiming their nation's third gold medal in as many events at the Diving. Mexico and Canada took silver and bronze respectively, while Great Britain's Tonia Couch and Sarah Barrow failed to end the host nation's half-century wait for a female Diving medallist at the Games, ending the contest in fifth.

Elsewhere, fifth seed Jo-Wilfried Tsonga of France won the longest three-set match in Olympic Tennis history as he came through 6-3 3-6 25-23 against Canada's Milos Raonic in three minutes short of four hours, and even Olympic spectators joined in with the record breaking on Day 4 as 70,584 people headed to Wembley Stadium to see Team GB's women's football team beat Brazil 1-0, the best ever attendance for a women's football match in the country. Team GB full-back Stephanie Houghton scored for the third successive game.

Germany's Michael Jung won the Eventing Individual Competition Olympic gold medal on his 30th birthday

France's Tony Estanguet won his third Olympic title in the Canoe Slalom (C1) at the Lee Valley White Water Centre, adding the gold medal to those he won in Sydney and Athens

# For the record

## Olympic records

**Shooting – men's Skeet**
Vincent Hancock (USA) 148

**Weightlifting – women's 63kg**
Maiya Maneza (Kazakhstan) 245kg

**Swimming – women's 200m Freestyle**
Allison Schmitt (USA) 1:53.61

**Swimming – women's 200m Individual Medley**
Shiwen Ye (China) 2:07.57

**'We are all being carried along on this wave of craziness. This is something we have never experienced in our careers and never will again. It's just not normal'**

*Great Britain Eventing Team Competition silver medallist William Fox-Pitt*

**Left:** Ruolin Chen and Hao Wang triumphed in the women's Synchronised 10m Platform

**Below far left:** Jae-Bum Kim of the Republic of Korea (in blue) overcame Germany's Ole Bischof in the men's Judo Half-Middleweight (73-81kg) final

**Below left:** NBA star Pau Gasol scores against Australia in Spain's 82-70 win in the men's Basketball

**Above right:** Allison Schmitt of the United States set a new Olympic record as she won the women's 200m Freestyle

**Below right:** France's Jo-Wilfried Tsonga (right) beat Milos Raonic of Canada 25-23 in the deciding set, the longest three-set match ever in Olympic Tennis

**Below:** Kazakhstan's Maiya Maneza set a new Olympic record in winning the women's Weightlifting 63kg title

## Team GB moment of the day

Great Britain went into the final day of the Eventing Team Competition in second place. Their brave gold medal challenge ultimately came up short, but Tina Cook's near-faultless Jumping round ensured the host nation held on to secure silver. It completed a remarkable journey for Cook's horse Miners Frolic, who suffered from a life-threatening illness in 2011. The triumph also marked a medal win for the Queen's granddaughter, Zara Phillips, and saw Mary King collect her third medal at the Games at the age of 51 – 11 years after the mother-of-two had broken

## Golden Games moment

Michael Phelps was already recognised as one of the greatest swimmers of all time but he cemented his place in Games history by becoming the most decorated Olympian of all time. The United States' victory in the 4 x 200m Freestyle Relay took Phelps' all-time medal tally to a staggering 19 (15 gold, two silver and two bronze), surpassing a 48-year-old record held by the Soviet Union's Larissa Latynina, who dominated female Gymnastics between 1956 and 1964. The Maryland-born swimmer picked up a silver earlier in the night to equal Latynina's record after South Africa's Chad le Clos beat him in the 200m Butterfly. ■

# Day 5

Wednesday, 1 August 2012

## Going for gold

**Canoe Slalom**
Kayak Single (K1)

**Cycling – Road**
Women's Time Trial • Men's Time Trial

**Diving**
Men's Synchronised 3m Springboard

**Fencing**
Men's Individual Epée • Women's Individual Sabre

**Gymnastics**
Men's Individual All-Around Competition

**Judo**
Women's Middleweight (63-70kg) • Men's Middleweight (81–90kg)

**Rowing**
Women's Pair • Women's Quadruple Sculls • Men's Eight

**Shooting**
Women's 25m Pistol

**Swimming**
Men's 200m Breaststroke • Women's 200m Butterfly • Men's 100m Freestyle • Women's 4 x 200m Freestyle Relay

**Table Tennis**
Women's Singles

**Weightlifting**
Women's 69kg • Men's 77kg

**Right:** Ecstatic fans welcome Bradley Wiggins back to Hampton Court Palace after his victory in the men's Road Cycling Time Trial made him Great Britain's most decorated Olympian

# Double delight

**In an action-packed Day 5, cyclist Bradley Wiggins completed an amazing year, the host nation earned their first gold medals and there were more record-breaking performances in the Weightlifting and at the Aquatics Centre.**

Cyclist Bradley Wiggins cemented his place in sporting history on Day 5 of London 2012 by becoming the first man to win the Tour de France and Olympic Games gold in the same year with an emphatic victory in the men's Time Trial.

His golden moment gave the Londoner the honour of overtaking Sir Steve Redgrave as Great Britain's most decorated Olympian of all time on seven medals, four of them gold. Wiggins was the penultimate of 37 riders to depart from Hampton Court Palace on a sunny afternoon and completed the 44km course in 50:39.54 to push Germany's reigning world champion Tony Martin into second place, while fellow Briton Chris Froome, who was runner-up to Wiggins in the Tour de France, took the bronze.

Wiggins showed no signs of fatigue following the opening day's Road Race and reached the first time check, at 7.3km trailing Martin by five seconds. He subsequently built up a head of steam to take the lead at the second time check, before enhancing his advantage at the third checkpoint, with 14.1km remaining. To the delight of the thousands of spectators who lined the streets, Wiggins eventually won by a mammoth 42 seconds to secure Britain's first ever men's Cycling Road gold medal.

The host nation's women, however, were unable to repeat the men's Time Trial success, with Lizzie Armitstead and Emma Pooley missing out on the medals. The United States' Kristin Armstrong successfully defended her Time Trial title, finishing the 29km route a full 15 seconds clear of the field. World champion Judith Arndt of Germany was placed second, while Russia's Olga Zabelinskaya claimed her second bronze of the Games.

Earlier in the day, Eton Dorney witnessed its first Victory Ceremony of the Games and the first to hear their national anthem were Team GB's Helen Glover and Heather Stanning, who dominated the final of the women's Pair to take Britain's first gold medal of London 2012 and a first ever Olympic title for the nation's female rowers. The result marked the culmination of a remarkable four years for the duo. Glover, who was once an aspiring Hockey player and cross-country runner, only took up Rowing in 2008, while Stannard took a break from army duties with the Royal Artillery to allow her to train full-time ahead of London 2012.

At the age of 40, Greg Searle returned to Olympic Rowing in search of a gold medal to add to the one he won at Barcelona 1992, but had

Men's Time Trial winner Bradley Wiggins shows off his gold medal, flanked by Germany's Tony Martin (left) and fellow Great Britain competitor Chris Froome

'To put in a performance like that nine days after the Tour and win another Olympic title, it is never, ever going to get any better than that'

*Olympic Time Trial champion Bradley Wiggins*

GBR

**Above:** Rowers Helen Glover (left) and Heather Stanning won Great Britain's first gold medal of the Games in the women's Pair event at Eton Dorney

**Left:** Michael Jamieson's silver in the 200m Breaststroke was Great Britain's first medal in the event for 20 years. Alongside him (in far lane) is winner Daniel Gyurta of Hungary

**Right:** United States cyclist Kristin Armstrong retained her Olympic title in the women's Time Trial

**Below:** Germany's winning Eight celebrate with their Olympic gold medals

to settle for a bronze after his men's Eight crew faded in the final stretch of a race won by favourites Germany. There was also a gold for Ukraine in the women's Quadruple Sculls, in which Britain's women were sixth.

The British medal rush continued at the Aquatics Centre, where Michael Jamieson secured silver to claim the country's first 200m Breaststroke podium finish since 1992, when Nick Gillingham took bronze. Third at the final turn, Jamieson and eventual winner Daniel Gyurta of Hungary went head to head over the last 50 metres, but the Athens silver medallist held off the British swimmer's challenge to break the world record by 0.03 seconds with a time of of 2:07.28. Jamieson's time of 2:07.43 was the fourth fastest in history.

China's Liuyang Jiao won gold in the women's 200m Butterfly, fending off a strong field to set a new Olympic record, before USA's Nathan Adrian dashed Australian James Magnussen's hopes of adding the Olympic title to his world crown, pipping him by one hundredth of a second in the 100m Freestyle. There was further success in the pool for the United States as its women's 4 x 200m Freestyle Relay team took gold in Olympic record pace and Rebecca Soni swam to a new world record in a semi-final for the women's 200m Breaststroke.

At the North Greenwich Arena in the men's Gymnastics, Kohei Uchimura added to Japan's silver medal in the Team Competition by winning gold in the Individual All-Around Competition. The three-time All-Around world champion, who won silver at Beijing 2008, scored 92.690 to see off German Marcel Nguyen, who took silver, with the United States' Danell Leyva in bronze, just under two points off the lead.

In addition to their Swimming gold, China continued their impressive start

to the Games by claiming a further three titles on Day 5. Kai Qin and Yutong Luo continued the country's march towards a clean sweep of Diving golds as the women's Synchronised 3m Springboard pair made it four out of four.

## Li turns tables

Meanwhile, the final of the women's Singles Table Tennis was an all-Chinese affair won by Xiaoxia Li, who sprung a surprise by beating reigning world champion Ning Ding, and Xiaojun Lu took first place in the men's 77kg Weightlifting, setting a new world record in the process with a total of 379kg.

The day's other Weightlifting title went to Jong Sim Rim of the Democratic People's Republic of Korea, who took gold in the women's 69kg category. The competition proved unpredictable with Rim's gold being confirmed on the penultimate lift, while body weight alone separated second, third and fourth place.

It was a successful day for DPR Korea, as teenager Jangmi Kim beat defending champion Ying Chen of China with her final round to win gold in the women's 25m Pistol

Shooting event and Jiyeon Kim took gold in the women's Individual Sabre Fencing.

The country also claimed a Judo gold thanks to Dae-Nam Song in the Middleweight (81–90kg) division, while France's Lucie Decosse won the women's Middleweight (63–70kg) title.

Day 5 also provided Venezuela with a moment of glory, as men's Individual Epée Fencing competitor Ruben Limardo won his nation's first gold medal since 1968 and only its second in the history of the Games, while there was joy for an athlete on their birthday as Italy's Daniele Molmenti claimed the Canoe Slalom Kayak Single (K1) title to celebrate turning 28.

In the Sailing at Weymouth and Portland it was a rest day for the Finn class and Star fleet, but Pavlos Kontides raced into contention for gold in the Laser class. The Cypriot enhanced his chances of securing a podium finish by finishing second and fourth in the day's races, with Australia's Andrew Murdoch and Tonci Stipanovic of Croatia securing victories. It gave Kontides a one-point lead over Australia's four-time world champion Tom Slingsby.

China's Liuyang Jiao on her way to winning the women's 200m Butterfly

Kohei Uchimura of Japan, in action on the parallel bars, added a gold medal in the Gymnastics Individual All-Around Competition to the three world championship titles he has won in the same event

London 2012

**Left:** Xiaoxia Li (far) beat reigning world champion Ning Ding in an all-Chinese final in the women's Table Tennis

**Above:** Ruben Limardo's Fencing gold medal in the men's Individual Epée was Venezuela's first since 1968 and only the country's second ever

**Above right:** DPR Korea teenager Jangmi Kim held her nerve to win the women's 25m Pistol Shooting

**Below right:** Lucie Decosse of France (in white) beat Germany's Kerstin Thiele to take gold in the women's Judo Middleweight (63–70kg)

**Below:** The scene off Weymouth and Portland where Pavlos Kontides of Cyprus took a narrow lead in the Laser series

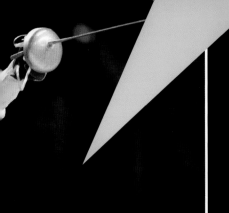

# For the record

## World records

**Swimming – men's 200m Breaststroke**
Daniel Gyurta (Hungary) 2:07.28

**Swimming – women's 200m Breaststroke**
Rebecca Soni (USA) 2:20.00

**Weightlifting – men's 77kg**
Xiaojun Lu (China) 379kg

## Olympic records

**Shooting – women's 25m Pistol**
Jangmi Kim (Republic of Korea) 591

**Swimming – women's 100m Freestyle**
Ranomi Kromowidjojo (Netherlands) 53.05

**Swimming – women's 200m Butterfly**
Liuyang Jiao (China) 2:04.06

**Swimming – women's 4 x 200m Freestyle Relay**
United States 7:42.92

## Team GB moment of the day

Sir Steve Redgrave has been regarded as Britain's greatest Olympian since winning his fifth consecutive gold medal at Sydney 2000, so it was always going to be a special moment when his overall medal tally of six was surpassed. That moment came for cyclist Bradley Wiggins on Day 5 of London 2012 as he emphatically claimed gold in the men's Time Trial to take his career medal tally to seven, including four golds.

Wiggins, an asthma sufferer, also wrote his name into the Cycling history books by becoming the first man to win both the Tour de France and Olympic gold in the same year and secured Britain's first ever medal in men's Road Cycling at the Games. Having been handed the honour of ringing the giant bell inside the Olympic Stadium to begin the Opening Ceremony, Wiggins provided one of the Games' more memorable moments when he collected his medal in the shadow of Hampton Court Palace.

## Golden Games moment

Prior to London 2012, Venezuela, a country with a population of almost 30 million people, had only one gold medal to its name – won by boxer Francisco Rodriguez at Mexico City 1968. However, on the first Wednesday of the Games, fencer Ruben Limardo wrote his name in his country's sporting history books when he defied the odds to take gold in the men's Individual Epée.

The world number 13 sparked scenes of unbridled joy among the South American nation's small contingent at the packed ExCeL after beating Norway's Bartosz Piasecki 15-10. Limardo, who put out world number five Max Heinzer in the last 16 and then Italy's reigning world champion Paolo Pizzo in the quarter-finals, was conceding more than 20cm in height to the 1.95m-tall, Polish-born Piasecki. But that did not matter as he raced into a 14-6 lead and, despite losing the next four points, Limardo cemented his place as a national hero by finishing the job to claim gold. ∎

# Day 6

## Going for gold

**Archery**
Women's Individual Competition

**Canoe Slalom**
Men's Canoe Double (C2) • Women's Kayak Single (K1)

**Cycling Track**
Women's Team Sprint • Men's Team Sprint

**Fencing**
Women's Team Foil

**Gymnastics**
Women's Individual All-Around Competition

**Judo**
Men's Half-Heavyweight (90-100kg) • Women's Half-Heavyweight (70-78kg)

**Rowing**
Men's Double Sculls • Men's Lightweight Four • Women's Eight

**Shooting**
Men's Double Trap

**Swimming**
Women's 200m Breaststroke • Men's 200m Backstroke • Men's 200m Individual Medley • Women's 100m Freestyle

**Table Tennis**
Men's Singles

**Right:** Sir Chris Hoy (back) won his fifth
Olympic gold medal as he and Great
Britain Cycling team-mates Jason Kenny
(middle) and Philip Hindes won the
Team Sprint in record-breaking style

# Awesome ability

**The history books had to be rewritten as Sir Chris Hoy and Michael Phelps struck gold once again on the track and in the pool respectively, while there were thrilling climaxes in the Canoe Slalom, Shooting and Judo.**

The Velodrome opened its doors for the first time and immediately witnessed some breathtaking performances as other events provided dramatic conclusions on a stunning day of action.

With the Road Cycling events coming to an end on the previous day, the Games' two-wheeled focus switched to the Velodrome. Track Cycling had proved to be a goldmine for Great Britain in Beijing four years earlier and the first day of events in London once again showcased the team's awesome ability. As part of the men's Team Sprint, Sir Chris Hoy cycled into the record books as he equalled Sir Steve Redgrave's record of five Olympic gold medals, doing so in world record-breaking fashion. After setting a new world best of 42.747 en route to the final, the trio, consisting of Hoy, Jason Kenny and Philip Hindes, clocked another world record in a stunning finale, finishing in 42.600. In a repeat of the Beijing 2008 final, France's Gregory Bauge, Michael D'Almeida and Kevin Sireau had to settle for silver, finishing in 43.013. Hoy rested his head on his handlebars as he was mobbed following his victory, before embarking on a lap of honour to the delight of the thousands of fans

who packed into the Olympic Park venue. There was further good news for Team GB as Ed Clancy, Steven Burke, Geraint Thomas and Peter Kennaugh laid down the gauntlet to their rivals by setting a new world record in the qualifying rounds of the men's Team Pursuit, while Germany took gold in the women's Team Sprint. They recorded a slower time than the Chinese team, but took over in first place when China were relegated for an overtaking infringement.

Earlier in the afternoon, the host nation had a remarkable time as they won two golds and a silver in the space of a few minutes. At Lee Valley

White Water Centre, Great Britain won its first ever Olympic gold medal in Canoe Slalom as they claimed gold and silver in the Canoe Double (C2). After narrowly squeezing their way into the final, Tim Baillie and Etienne Stott were first to go and laid down a marker of 106.41 seconds. After subsequent runs by China, Poland and France failed to threaten the British pair's position at the top, it was the turn of legendary Slovakian twins Pavol and Peter Hochschorner, who had won gold at the previous three Olympic Games. But they failed to live up to their reputation as their run of 108.28 fell short of Stott and

Jason Kenny, Philip Hindes and Chris Hoy show off their gold medals

**❝ I don't think surreal really covers it. It's crazy. I think I will bask in the happy, strange glow for a few days ❞**

*Great Britain's Tim Baillie who, with Etienne Stott, won gold in the Canoe Double (C2)*

**Above:** Farmer's son Peter Wilson won Shooting gold for Great Britain after a tense finish to the Double Trap final

**Below:** Rebecca Soni set a new world record in winning the women's 200m Breaststroke

**Right:** China's Jike Zhang added the men's Table Tennis Singles gold medal to past successes in the World Cup and World Championship

**Bottom:** Tim Baillie (3) and Etienne Stott lead a British one-two in the Canoe Double (C2)

Baillie's time – meaning Team GB were guaranteed a gold medal with the second British pairing of Richard Hounslow and David Florence the last out on the unforgiving course. The duo had the opportunity to put Britain on the top two steps of the podium and duly posted a time of 106.77 to take silver, narrowly missing out on gold, and pushing the Hochschorner twins into third place in the process. The result sparked joyous scenes as a jubilant home crowd gave them a standing ovation. In the women's Kayak Single (K1), meanwhile, France's Emilie Fer won gold ahead of Australian teenager Jessica Fox in second, with Spain's Maialen Chourraut taking bronze.

At The Royal Artillery Barracks, shooter Peter Wilson was aiming for his own piece of history in the men's Double Trap. The 25-year-old farmer's son from Dorset, who was the world record holder and world number two going into the Games, was three points ahead going into the afternoon's final, which he led from start to finish. In a tense final shoot-out, Wilson missed five shots but his opponents could not capitalise and left the Briton needing one hit from the final two targets. Wilson nailed both before falling to his knees in relief, finishing two clear of Sweden's Hakan Dahlby with a total score of 188 out of 200 shots.

London's ExCeL was the location for a remarkable march to the final for Great Britain's Gemma Gibbons in the women's Half-Heavyweight (70-78kg) Judo competition. Gibbons, who is coached by Britain's last medallist in the sport, Kate Howey, disposed of world champion Audrey Tcheumeo of France in eye-catching fashion with an ippon throw in extra time to reach the final before Kayla Harrison claimed a narrow victory by two yukos, to secure the United States' first ever Judo Olympic title. Russia's Tagir Khaibulaev took gold in the men's Half-Heavyweight (90-100kg) division.

## Rowing thriller

Britain's rowers once again found themselves on the podium on Day 6 as the men's Lightweight Four crew took silver in a race that was neck-and-neck all the way to the finish line. As Denmark faded into the bronze medal position late on, South Africa surged through the field to win the country's first ever Rowing gold. In the day's other races at Eton Dorney, New Zealand won gold in the men's Double Sculls and the United States retained their Olympic title in the women's Eight.

On another great night for the United States at the Aquatics Centre, Michael Phelps extended his record as the most decorated Olympian of all time by winning his first solo gold of the Games in the men's 200m Individual Medley to take his tally to 20 medals, compatriot Rebecca Soni broke the world record on her way to winning the women's 200m Breaststroke and Tyler Clary was victorious in the men's 200m Backstroke. The night's other gold medal went to Ranomi Kromowidjojo of the Netherlands in the women's 100m Freestyle.

Italy's so-called 'dream team' of six-time Olympic gold-medallist Valentina Vezzali, Elisa Di Francisca – now a double gold medal-winner at London 2012 – and new world number one Arianna Errigo were victorious in Fencing's women's Team Foil competition with a 45-31 win over Russia in the final. China continued their quest to take all four Table Tennis titles with victory in the men's Singles for Jike Zhang, who completed a career grand slam having previously won the World Championships and World Cup. In the Gymnastics women's Individual All-Around Competition, the USA's Gabrielle Douglas – nicknamed the 'Flying Squirrel' – clinched top spot with a total of 62.232 points, while the Republic of Korea had cause for celebration at Lord's Cricket Ground, where Bo Bae Ki won the women's Archery Individual Competition.

Great Britain (3) were silver medallists in the men's Lightweight Four behind winners South Africa (5)

Gemma Gibbons of Great Britain (in blue) had an amazing run to the final of the women's Judo Half-Heavyweight (70-78kg), before having to settle for silver after defeat against Kayla Harrison (in white) of the United States

**Above left:** Gabrielle Douglas won the women's Gymnastics Individual All-Around Competition

**Above right :** Valentina Vezzali won a sixth Olympic Fencing gold medal as part of Italy's line-up in the women's Team Foil

**Left:** Republic of Korea's Bo Bae Ki (right) beat Mexico's Aida Roman Arroyo in the women's Archery Individual final

**Right:** Australia's James Clarke in action in the 13-9 defeat to Spain in their men's Group A Water Polo match

**Below:** Michael Phelps (centre left) took his tally to 20 Olympic Games medals when he won the men's 200m Individual Medley

# For the record

## World records

**Track Cycling – women's Team Sprint**
China 32.422

**Track Cycling – men's Team Pursuit**
Great Britain 3:52.499

**Track Cycling – men's Team Sprint**
Great Britain 42.600

**Swimming – women's 200m Breaststroke**
Rebecca Soni (USA) 2:19.59

## Olympic records

**Swimming – men's 200m Backstroke**
Tyler Clary (USA) 1:53.41

**Swimming – women's 100m Freestyle**
Ranomi Kromowidjojo (Netherlands) 53.00

## Team GB moment of the day

All the talk in the lead-up to London 2012 was about Great Britain's medal prospects in sports such as Cycling, Rowing and Athletics, but Day 6 saw the hosts spring a surprise by dominating the men's Canoe Double (C2) event to win its first ever gold medal in Canoe Slalom. After scraping into the final by qualifying in sixth position in the semi-final, Etienne Stott and Tim Baillie were first down the course, setting a time that would not be matched by the rest of the field, not even the legendary Hochschorner twins, Peter and Pavol, who had won gold at the previous three Olympic Games.

By the time the second British pairing of Richard Hounslow and David Florence had their turn, Team GB were guaranteed an Olympic title. That duo missed out on gold by a fraction, but ensured the country witnessed an unexpected gold and silver win in Canoe Slalom. Jubilant scenes ensued as th canoeists, along with members of their back-up team, jumped into the water to the delight of a capacity crowd at Lee Valley White Water Centre.

## Golden Games moment

The United States came full circle on their remarkable six-year winning streak with victory in the women's Eight Rowing on Day 6 of London 2012, continuing a run that began at Eton Dorney in the 2006 World Championships. Despite a number of line-up changes, the performances had remained consistently dominant and this medal-winning performance continue that form as the team led from start to finish.

The Olympic title was the country's third in the event, equalling a record hel by Romania and the former East Germany. The United States' closest rivals for gold were neighbours Canada, who had 52-year-old Lesley Thompson-Willie competing at her sixth Games since making her debut in 1984 – among their crew. Canada took silver, finishing little more than a second behind five-time world champions United States, while the Netherlands were forced to settle fo the bronze medal. ∎

# Day 7

## Going for gold

**Archery**
Men's Individual Competition

**Athletics**
Men's Shot Put • Women's 10,000m

**Badminton**
Mixed Doubles

**Cycling – Track**
Men's Team Pursuit • Women's Keirin

**Fencing**
Men's Team Sabre

**Gymnastics – Trampoline**
Men's Individual Competition

**Judo**
Women's Heavyweight (over 78kg) • Men's Heavyweight
(over 100kg)

**Rowing**
Men's Quadruple Sculls • Men's Pair • Women's Double
Sculls • Men's Single Sculls

**Shooting**
Men's 50m Rifle Prone • Men's 25m Rapid Fire Pistol

**Swimming**
Women's 200m Backstroke • Men's 100m Butterfly •
Women's 800m Freestyle • Men's 50m Freestyle

**Weightlifting**
Women's 75kg • Men's 85kg

**Right:** For the second day running, Great
Britain dominated in the Velodrome, where
the Team Pursuit quartet followed in the
wheeltracks of the Team Sprint and won
another gold medal

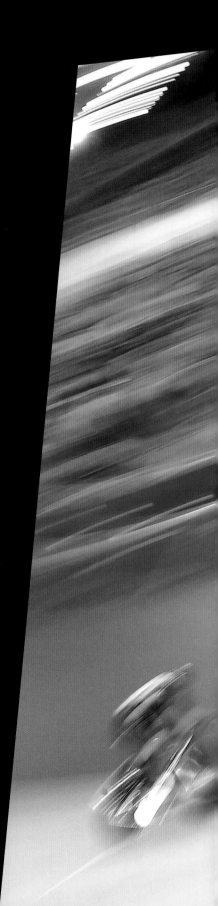

# Another gear

**On a day when the magnificent Olympic Stadium saw its first action, there were 22 gold medals on offer in 11 different sports around the Games and a host of nations triumphed as the thrills came thick and fast once again.**

One of the busiest 24 hours of the Games so far saw athletes from 12 different nations take their place at the top of the podium as London 2012 stepped up another gear.

While the Olympic Stadium opened its doors for the first time since the Opening Ceremony, the day's early medal action got under way at Eton Dorney, where Germany were first to taste Rowing victory by taking gold in the men's Quadruple Sculls with a stunning win over silver medallists Croatia. That was followed by a dominant display from the New Zealand duo of Hamish Bond and Eric Murray in the men's Pair. Having won the World Championships in 2009, 2010 and 2011, Olympic gold cemented the Kiwis' place at the top of their sport.

There was relief and delight in equal measure for Great Britain's Katherine Grainger, who, along with partner Anna Watkins, rowed to gold in the women's Double Sculls. Grainger became the first British female to win a medal at three consecutive Games in 2008, but was still searching for an elusive gold after claiming silver on each occasion. The pair stormed to an emphatic victory and the relief was plain for all to see as they crossed the line – Grainger punching the air before falling into an embrace with Watkins. New Zealand then bagged their second gold of the morning when five-time world champion Mahe Drysdale won the men's Single Sculls, crossing the line ahead of Lassi Karonen of Sweden and Great Britian's Alan Campbell, who barely had the power to stand following the race, having given his all to win a bronze medal. For Drysdale, it made up for the disappointment of four years earlier, when he finished third having been affected by illness in the lead-up to the final at Beijing 2008.

At The Royal Artillery Barracks, shooter Sergei Martynov of Belarus ran away with the gold medal in the men's 50m Rifle Prone with a world-record score of 705.5, while Cuba's Leuris Pupo equalled the Olympic record in the men's 25m Rapid Fire Pistol to deny world number one Alexei Klimov the victory.

The afternoon continued to deliver a string of stunning performances, including that of Chinese pairing Nan Zhang and Yunlei Zhao, who took the first Badminton gold of London 2012 with victory over compatriots Chen Xu and Jin Ma in the Mixed Doubles. Day 7 also saw

Victoria Pendleton celebrates winning the women's Keirin

**❛A lot of people thought I'd passed my best and I just wanted to prove them wrong, so this does feel pretty good❜**

*Great Britain cyclist Victoria Pendleton after winning the women's Keirin*

**Above:** Katherine Grainger (front) and Anna Watkins won the women's Double Sculls at Eton Dorney, ending Grainger's sequence of silver medals at three successive Games

**Below:** The honour of winning London 2012's first gold medal in the Olympic Stadium went to Tomasz Majewski of Poland, who triumphed in the men's Shot Put

**Right:** Five-time world champion Teddy Riner of France justified being favourite when he won the gold medal in the men's Judo Heavyweight (over 100kg) final

the trampolinists spring into action and a win for Dong Dong in the men's event meant it was turning out to be another golden day for China.

Kazakhstan's gold rush continued as Svetlana Podobedova notched their fourth Olympic title of the Games. The 26-year-old held off the threat of her two Russian rivals to take gold in the women's 75kg Weightlifting, while the men's 85kg title went to Poland's Adrian Edward Zielinski.

History was made in the Archery at Lord's Cricket Ground as the Republic of Korea ended their long wait for a first Olympic title in the men's Individual Competition – Jin Hyek Oh defeating Japan's Takaharu Furukawa 7-1 in the final. France's Teddy Riner raised no eyebrows by winning gold in the men's Heavyweight (over 100kg) Judo at ExCeL. The 23-year-old went into the Games as a five-time world champion and proved too strong for Russian Alexander Mikhaylin in the final. After going 12 years without a Judo medal at the Games, Great Britain were only made to wait 24 hours for the next one, as Karina Bryant took bronze in a Heavyweight (over 78kg) event won by Japan's Mika Sugimoto.

As the evening progressed, attention switched to the Velodrome,

where Great Britain once again proved superior. With two gold medals on offer, the host nation's men's Team Pursuit squad set the ball rolling by taking gold in world record-breaking fashion. Ed Clancy, Geraint Thomas, Steven Burke and Peter Kennaugh set a new best time for the second consecutive night as they cycled to victory over Australia in 3:51.659. Great Britain's golden day continued as Victoria Pendleton cycled to gold in the women's Keirin, asserting Team GB's two-wheeled dominance with a third Track Cycling title out of a potential four for the country so far.

## Five-star Koreans

Prior to the Games, the Republic of Korea had only ever won three Fencing medals, but their victory in the men's Team Sabre was their fifth of the week and second gold – with their triumph coming despite being ranked sixth of the eight teams involved.

The United States continued to rule the pool on the seventh night of action at the Aquatics Centre. Missy Franklin set the standard in the women's 200m Backstroke by claiming her third gold medal of the Games in a world-record time, before compatriot Michael Phelps

added to his incredible haul of medals with victory in the men's 100m Butterfly, beating Russia's Evgeny Korotyshkin and South Africa's Chad le Clos into silver and bronze respectively, to take his tally to 21. A surprise came when 15-year-old Katie Ledecky stormed clear of the field to take gold in the women's 800m Freestyle ahead of Spain's Mireia Belmonte Garcia and Britain's reigning champion Rebecca Adlington. Florent Manaudou closed the night by winning France's fourth Swimming gold of the week with victory in the men's 50m Freestyle.

The final two gold medals of a memorable day of action came on the opening night of events in the Olympic Stadium, where Poland took the first on offer as Tomasz Majewski fended off the competition in the Shot Put with a best throw of 21.89m. The night was brought to a close with the women's 10,000m final, where Ethiopia's defending champion Tirunesh Dibaba posted a final lap of 62.08 to surge clear of her Kenyan rivals on her way to glory.

In some of the day's other events, Jessica Ennis set a world best in the Heptathlon's 100m hurdles as she held an overnight lead of 184 points, Iain Percy and Andrew Simpson guaranteed Team GB a medal in Sailing's Star event and Andy Murray set up a repeat of the 2012 Wimbledon final against Roger Federer with victory over Serbia's Novak Djokovic. The Swiss ace came through an epic encounter of his own to reach the gold medal match, beating Argentina's Juan Martin Del Potro 19-17 in the final set of a 4h26m contest on Centre Court. There was disappointment for Team GB's women's Football team, however, as they went out at the hands of Canada, who joined Japan, France and the United States in the last four of the competition.

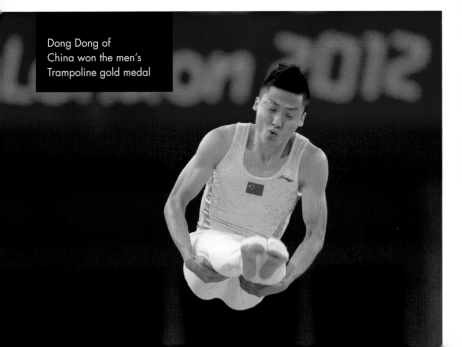

Dong Dong of China won the men's Trampoline gold medal

Ethiopian athlete
Tirunesh Dibaba
successfully
defended her
Olympic title
by winning
the women's
10,000m in the
Olympic Stadium

# For the record

## World records

**Track Cycling – women's Team Pursuit**
Great Britain 3:15.659

**Track Cycling – men's Team Pursuit**
Great Britain 3:51.659

**Swimming – women's 200m Backstroke**
Missy Franklin (USA) 2:04.06

**Shooting – men's 50m Rifle Prone**
Sergei Martynov (Belarus) 705.5

## Olympic records

**Weightlifting – women's 75kg**
Natalya Zabolotnaya (Russian Federation) 291kg

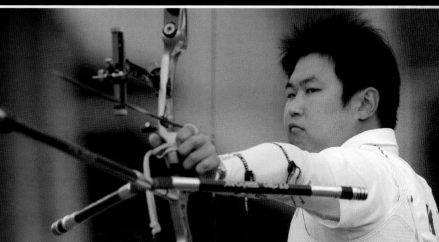

**Far left top:** Mahé Drysdale of New Zealand added Olympic gold in the men's Single Sculls to his five world championship titles

**Far left bottom:** Jessica Ennis made the ideal start to the Heptathlon in the 100m hurdles

**Left:** There was an all-Chinese gold medal match in the Badminton Mixed Doubles, where Nan Zhang and Yunlei Zhao (in yellow) overcame compatriots Chen Xu and Jin Ma to take the sport's first title of London 2012 at Wembley Arena

**Above:** Sergei Martynov of Belarus set a new world record to win the men's 50m Rifle Prone event

**Below:** Jin Hyek Oh won the Republic of Korea's first men's Archery Individual gold medal

## Team GB moment of the day

The Olympic Games had always been a case of so near but yet so far for rower Katherine Grainger. After winning her third consecutive silver medal at Beijing 2008, Grainger even thought about giving up the sport altogether. However, Day 7 of London 2012 saw Grainger fulfil a lifelong dream alongside partner Anna Watkins – with whom she had won two world titles – in the women's Double Sculls. Grainger said: 'Any Olympic medal is a phenomenal achievement in itself. Having had three in the past of, for me, not the right colour, it became the one I wanted to complete the collection.'

## Golden Games moment

The opening night of Athletics at the Olympic Stadium was brought to a close by a thrilling performance from Ethiopia's Tirunesh Dibaba in the women's 10,000m. The 27-year-old, who won the distance double at Beijing 2008 – the first woman to do so – saw off the Kenyan duo of Sally Kipyego and Vivian Cheruiyot with a final-lap burst to win by more than five seconds. Dibaba's sprint finish saw her complete the last lap in just 62.08 seconds, leaving the rest of the field in her wake. The medal was Ethiopia's first of London 2012 and signalled the beginning of a week when the country would hope to make their mark on the track. ∎

# Day 8

## Saturday, 4 August 2012

## Going for gold

**Athletics**
Men's 20km Race Walk • Women's Discus Throw • Men's Long Jump • Women's Heptathlon • Men's 10,000m • Women's 100m

**Badminton**
Women's Doubles • Women's Singles

**Cycling – Track**
Women's Team Pursuit

**Fencing**
Women's Team Epée

**Gymnastics – Trampoline**
Women's Individual Competition

**Rowing**
Men's Four • Women's Lightweight Double Sculls • Men's Lightweight Double Sculls • Women's Single Sculls

**Shooting**
Women's 50m Rifle 3 Positions • Women's Trap

**Swimming**
Women's 50m Freestyle • Men's 1500m Freestyle • Women's 4 x 100m Medley Relay • Men's 4 x 100m Medley Relay

**Tennis**
Women's Singles • Men's Doubles

**Triathlon**
Women's Triathlon

**Weightlifting**
Men's 94kg

**Right:** Great Britain's Jessica Ennis might have felt the weight of expectation on her shoulders but delivered the goods with a brilliant finish to the final event, the 800m, to seal victory in the Heptathlon

# Super Saturday

## 4 August 2012

**Team GB won an incredible six gold medals as 'Super Saturday' well and truly belonged to the host nation on a day when Jessica Ennis, the poster girl of London 2012, fulfilled her destiny in fine style.**

Saturday 4 August was always going to be one of the hottest tickets of London 2012 and it lived up to its billing as Jessica Ennis stole the show with Day 8 bringing unrivalled glory for the host nation.

Few athletes had to deal with the levels of hype endured by the heptathlete in the lead-up to the Games but if she was feeling the weight of a nation's expectations, she did not show it. Her every appearance was greeted with deafening cheers from the 80,000 crowd inside the Olympic Stadium, but she set about her business with remarkable composure. The Sheffield-born star led going into the second day of the event, having set a new world record in the 100m hurdles a day earlier, and following a solid performance in the long jump, Ennis took a huge stride towards gold with a personal best in the javelin. With a lead of 188 points and gold a near-certainty, the 800m served as a lap – or two – of honour for Britain's newest hero, but she did not rest on her laurels and produced another stunning performance to finish in first place. The first playing of the British national anthem in the Olympic Stadium was met with passionate singing by thousands of partisan spectators, sparking tears in the eyes of the 26-year-old, who was overcome with the enormity of her achievement.

On what was a sensational night for Team GB, Greg Rutherford was crowned Long Jump champion. Rutherford's winning leap of 8.31m came at precisely the same time as Ennis was being introduced before her 800m race, triggering a moment of euphoria in the stands. The 25-year-old put years of injury woes behind him to become the first Briton since Lynn Davies in 1964 to win Long Jump gold at the Games.

Incredibly it got even better for the British fans as Mo Farah then produced a stunning display in the men's 10,000m to make it a truly golden night for the host nation. With a perfectly judged race, Farah disposed of his opponents in the final lap as he surged away from the rest of the field. With a stunned look on his face, the 29-year-old collapsed to the ground after crossing the finish line before being greeted on the track by his seven-year-old stepdaughter Rihanna and pregnant wife Tania. He then headed off on a lap of honour to enjoy the adulation of the crowd.

Shelly-Ann Fraser-Pryce of Jamaica retained her women's 100m Olympic title, winning by just 0.03 in the final

**❛ I can't believe I've had the opportunity to come to my first Games in London and won an Olympic gold medal. It's unbelievable ❜**

*Great Britain's Jessica Ennis after winning the Heptathlon*

**Above:** Greg Rutherford played his part in a remarkable night at the Olympic Stadium for the host nation by winning the men's Long Jump

**Below:** Great Britain continued their fine form at Eton Dorney when Andrew Triggs Hodge, Pete Reed, Tom James and Alex Gregory won the men's Four

**Right:** Jessica Ennis shows off her Heptathlon gold. With a clear lead going into the final event, the 800m was a near formality in front of a jubilant home crowd

**Below right:** China's Ding Chen set a new Olympic record as he won the men's 20km Race Walk, which finished on The Mall in central London

In the night's other Athletics events, Jamaica's Shelly-Ann Fraser-Pryce defended her title from Beijing 2008 in a thrilling women's 100m final which saw six sprinters post times of under 11 seconds, while Croatia's Sandra Perkovic took gold in the women's Discus Throw. Meanwhile, beyond the Stadium, China's Ding Chen powered to gold in the men's 20km Race Walk on The Mall.

Away from Athletics, it was the final day of Rowing at Eton Dorney, where Team GB confirmed London 2012 as their most successful regatta ever by winning two golds and a silver. In the first final of the day, the host nation produced a sensational performance to beat Australia and win gold in the men's Four. Andrew Triggs Hodge, Pete Reed, Tom James and Alex Gregory led from the start to secure Britain's fourth consecutive Olympic title in the event.

In the very next race, the expression of shock on the faces of Sophie Hosking and Katherine Copeland was priceless after their victory in the women's Lightweight Double Sculls final, while Zac Purchase and Mark Hunter backed that up with silver in the same event for men in a race won by Denmark's Mads Rasmussen and Rasmus Quist. Miroslava Knapkova of the Czech Republic took the final Rowing gold of the Games with victory in the women's Single Sculls.

The morning of Day 8 also saw the female triathletes getting their chance to shine and, after swimming, cycling and running their way through London's Hyde Park, Nicola Spirig of Switzerland edged out Sweden's Lisa Norden in a photo-finish as the event came to a dramatic conclusion. In the Shooting, Italy's Jessica Rossi was close to perfection in the women's Trap as the 20-year-old policewoman hit 99 of her 100 clay targets to smash the world record, while the United States' Jamie Lynn Gray was a runaway winner of the women's 50m

Rifle 3 Positions by setting a new Olympic record of 691.9.

China asserted their Badminton dominance by moving one step closer to a clean sweep of the gold medals. Xuerui Li defeated her illustrious opponent Yihan Wang in an all-Chinese affair to claim the women's Singles title and Qing Tian and Yunlei Zhao took victory in the women's Doubles. The women's Trampoline Individual Competition at the North Greenwich Arena saw Canada's Rosannagh MacLennan win gold ahead of reigning champion Wenna He of China.

## Serena's golden double

Over at Wimbledon, Serena Williams became the first woman to complete the so-called 'golden slam' in both Singles and Doubles – having won two previous Doubles titles with sister Venus – with a convincing 6-1 6-0 victory over Maria Sharapova in the women's Singles final, while USA compatriots Bob and Mike Bryan took gold in the men's Doubles.

At the Velodrome, Great Britain once again proved their Track Cycling prowess by dominating the women's Team Pursuit competition. Joanna Rowsell, Dani King and Laura Trott remarkably achieved their sixth world record in a row in beating

the USA by over five seconds in the final, before spectators broke into a rendition of *Hey Jude* under the watchful eye of Sir Paul McCartney moments after the Victory Ceremony.

It was the end of an era at the Aquatics Centre as Michael Phelps competed in his final Olympic Games race and the Baltimore swimmer fittingly signed off with gold number 18 – his 22nd medal in total – in the 4 x 100m Medley Relay. The Netherlands' Ranomi Kromowidjojo added to her London 2012 medal haul with victory in the women's 50m Freestyle, before China's Sun Yang swam to victory in the men's 1500m Freestyle in a world record time of 14:31:02. The records continued to fall as the United States set a new world best in the women's 4 x 100m Medley Relay.

In some of the day's later events at ExCeL, China took gold in the women's Team Epée Fencing, while Kazakhstan's Ilya Ilyin won gold in the men's 94kg Weightlifting. On a day packed full of drama, Oscar Pistorius became the first double amputee to compete at an Olympic Games when qualifying for the 400m semi-finals while in the men's Football, Team GB were beaten on penalties as Korea joined Brazil, Japan and Mexico in the semi-finals.

Nicola Spirig of Switzerland edged out Sweden's Lisa Norden in a photo-finish in the women's Triathlon

Great Britain's Mo Farah has the finishing line – and Olympic gold – in his sights as he sprints away on the final straight to win the men's 10,000m

**Above:** Canada's Rosannagh MacLennan won gold in the women's Trampoline

**Left:** Xuerui Li's delight is clear after winning another all-Chinese final in the Badminton women's Singles

**Below:** Sandra Perkovic won gold for Croatia in the women's Discus Throw with a distance of 69.11

**Above right:** Sophie Hosking and Katherine Copeland surprised even themselves with victory in the women's Lightweight Double Sculls at Eton Dorney

**Right:** Serena Williams added women's Tennis Singles gold to her set of grand slams

**Below right:** Double amputee Oscar Pistorius qualified for the semi-finals in the men's 400m

# For the record

## World records

**Track Cycling – women's Team Pursuit**
Great Britain 3:14.051

**Shooting – women's Trap**
Jessica Rossi (Italy) 99

**Swimming – men's 1500m Freestyle**
Sun Yang (China) 14:31.02

**Swimming – women's 4 x 100m Medley Relay**
USA 3:52.05

**Weightlifting – men's 94kg**
Ilya Ilyin (Kazakhstan) 418kg

## Olympic records

**Athletics – men's 20km Race Walk**
Ding Chen (China) 1:18:46

**Shooting – women's 50m Rifle 3 Positions**
Jamie Lynn Gray (USA) 691.9

**Swimming – women's 50m Freestyle**
Ranomi Kromowidjojo (Netherlands) 24.05

## Team GB moment of the day

The British public were left catching their breath on a day when the tag of 'Super Saturday' was truly deserved, with the host nation enjoying its most successful single day at an Olympic Games for more than a century. After golds at Eton Dorney and the Velodrome, it was Team GB's track and field stars who delivered a blockbuster evening of entertainment. Within the space of 45 minutes, three new British Olympic champions were crowned in front of a 80,000-strong crowd.

Jessica Ennis lived up to the hype by delivering a series of brilliant performances in the Heptathlon and it seemed the night had reached its crescendo as she crossed the finish line in her final event, but moments later Greg Rutherford took Long Jump gold and the stage was set for Mo Farah to make it a hat-trick of golds. The 29-year-old did not disappoint and claimed a sixth British gold of the day to send the Olympic Stadium into raptures.

## Golden Games moment

Serena Williams has been a dominant force in women's Tennis for more than a decade and, on Day 8 of London 2012, hit a new milestone by completing a Singles 'golden slam' – the Olympic Games and all four grand slams – to go with the Doubles equivalent she already had with sister Venus.

The 30-year-old returned to the site of her 2012 Wimbledon victory to take on Russia's Maria Sharapova in the gold medal match on the famous Centre Court and romped to a 6-0 6-1 win. Williams said afterwards: 'I would have been happy whether I'd got silver or gold, because it's such a great achievement to get on that medal stand. But obviously I've won a gold. It's a big moment.' ∎

# Day 9

Sunday, 5 August 2012

## Going for gold

**Athletics**
Women's Marathon • Women's Triple Jump • Men's Hammer Throw •
Women's 400m • Men's 3000m Steeplechase • Men's 100m

**Badminton**
Men's Doubles • Men's Singles

**Cycling Track**
Men's Omnium

**Diving**
Women's 3m Springboard

**Fencing**
Men's Team Foil

**Gymnastics**
Men's Floor Competition • Women's Vault Competition •
Men's Pommel Horse Competition

**Sailing**
Men's Star • Men's Finn

**Shooting**
Men's 50m Pistol

**Tennis**
Men's Singles • Women's Doubles • Mixed Doubles

**Weightlifting**
Women's +75kg

**Wrestling Greco-Roman**
Men's 55kg • Men's 74kg

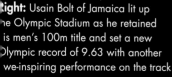

**Right:** Usain Bolt of Jamaica lit up
the Olympic Stadium as he retained
his men's 100m title and set a new
Olympic record of 9.63 with another
awe-inspiring performance on the track

# A night to remember
## 5 August 2012

**On one of the most eagerly-anticipated nights of the Games, Usain Bolt proved again he is the man for the big occasion by storming to victory in the men's 100m to retain his Olympic title and round off another dramatic day.**

It was the ticket that everybody wanted in the build-up to London 2012 and the men's 100m final did not disappoint as Usain Bolt created another magical Olympic moment that will be talked about for years to come.

On another memorable day, when 23 gold medals were handed out, the focus switched to the Olympic Stadium to see if the Jamaican superstar could repeat his heroics from the Beijing 2008 Games and, up against a stellar line-up of the world's fastest men, Bolt struck in majestic fashion to cement his legendary status. An all-time classic looked on the cards after seven of the eight qualifiers ran under 10 seconds in the semi-finals, but what transpired was even more spectacular than anyone could have imagined. Bolt made a slow start, but the tall sprinter moved through the gears and left his rivals trailing in his wake to cross the line in 9.63 – the second fastest time in history and better than the time he produced when winning the 100m title four years earlier. He had to dig deep to retain his Olympic crown as teammate Yohan Blake pushed him all the way to finish in second in a personal best-equalling 9.75. Justin Gatlin of the USA took bronze in 9.79 in a race where the first seven runners came home in under 10 seconds. The chances of all eight doing so for the first time ever were ruined when Asafa Powell, the third Jamaican in the final, suffered an injury just before the line and limped home.

There was more thrilling action on the track earlier in the night when Londoner Christine Ohuruogu claimed silver in the women's 400m behind Sanya Richards-Ross of the USA. Ohuruogu, who was raised less than a mile from the Olympic Park in Stratford, was the defending champion, but after a hard time with injuries since 2008 her return to form was a welcome sight as the British athlete produced her trademark late charge to finish second behind the impressive Richards-Ross. In the night's other Athletics finals, Kenya won the men's 3000m Steeplechase title for an eighth Games running as Athens 2004 champion Ezekiel Kemboi regained his crown, Olga Rypakova of Kazakhstan claimed women's Triple Jump gold with a leap of 14.98m and Hungary's Krisztian Pars won the Hammer Throw with 80.59m. Away from the Olympic Stadium, Ethiopia's Tiki Gelana revelled in the rain on the streets of London as she claimed a surprise victory in the women's Marathon in what was her first ever major championship, setting a new Olympic record of 2:23.07 in the process.

It was another wonderful day for Team GB as both Andy Murray and Ben Ainslie made history for the host

Usain Bolt strikes a familar pose as he celebrates his 100m victory

> **My coach told me to stop worrying about the start and concentrate on the end because that's my best. I knew what I needed to do**

*Usain Bolt on retaining his Olympic 100m title*

**Above:** Great Britain's Ben Ainslie celebrates becoming the most successful sailor in Olympic history after he won the Finn class to claim gold at a fourth successive Games

**Left:** The women's Marathon, won in an Olympic record time by Tiki Gelana, passed by a number of London's iconic landmarks, including the Houses of Parliament

**Below:** The men's 3000m Steeplechase title went to Kenya for an eighth successive Games thanks to Ezekiel Kemboi

nation. Murray won Britain's first men's Singles title in Olympic Tennis since 1908 and in doing so gained revenge on Switzerland's Roger Federer for his heartbreaking loss four weeks earlier in the Wimbledon final. His victory on Centre Court came in emphatic style as the 6-2 6-1 6-4 scoreline was Federer's heaviest ever defeat at the All England Club and denied him the chance of completing the career 'golden slam'. Murray had little time to celebrate, however, as he prepared to go for double gold in the Mixed Doubles less than an hour later. But he and Laura Robson lost 2-6 6-3 (10-8) to Belarus' Max Mirnyi and Victoria Azarenka. Also at Wimbledon, the USA's Serena Williams secured her second gold of London 2012 as she won the women's Doubles title with sister Venus for a third time.

Ainslie claimed his own special place in the record books by becoming the most successful sailor in Olympic history after securing a fourth successive gold medal. The 35-year-old replaced Denmark's Paul Elvstrom as the Games' most decorated sailor after triumphing on home waters off Weymouth and Portland. Ainslie faced fierce resistance throughout the regatta from Elvstrom's countryman Jonas Hogh-Christensen, but he

managed to finish ahead of the Dane in the crucial medal race of the Finn class and that was enough to claim overall victory. In the day's other medal race, Britain's Iain Percy and Andrew Simpson had to settle for silver in a Star class competition won by Sweden's Fredrik Loof and Max Salminen.

## Badminton clean sweep

China completed a clean sweep of gold medals in the Badminton as top seeds Yun Cai and Haifeng Fu won the men's Doubles, while Dan Lin defended his Olympic Singles crown with another thrilling victory over arch-rival Wei Chong Lee of Malaysia, digging deep in a compelling third game to win 15-21 21-10 21-19 in a repeat of the 2008 final. China also continued their quest to win all the Diving titles on offer as Minxia Wu won their fifth gold with her victory in the women's 3m Springboard, taking her career tally to a record-equalling six golds.

The Chinese were celebrating further success as Lulu Zhou won the women's +75kg Weightlifting by setting a new world record, while Kai Zou won gold in the men's Floor Competition on a day of individual apparatus finals in the Artistic Gymnastics. Louis Smith

was denied the gold on a tie-break with Hungary's Krisztian Berki in the Pommel Horse Competition, with the British gymnast losing due to a lower execution score after both were awarded 16.066 for their routines. Smith was joined on the podium by 19-year-old Max Whitlock, who claimed bronze, as the duo each secured their second medal of the Games following their third place in the Team Competition. In the women's Vault Competition, Romania's Sandra Raluca Izbasa narrowly saw off world champion McKayla Maroney of the USA to win gold.

Elsewhere, Team GB won another medal in the Velodrome as Ed Clancy took the bronze behind Denmark's Lasse Hansen in the men's six-event Omnium, Jongoh Jin of the Republic of Korea completed an amazing fightback to retain his men's 50m Pistol title, while the men's Fencing Foil Team competition was won by Italy. The first Greco-Roman ling gold of the Games went to Iran's Hamid Soryan in the 55kg division, while in the 74kg event the title went to Russia's Roman Vlasov. Day 9 also saw history made in the Boxing as women competed for the first time with Russia's Elena Savelyeva the first female winner of an Olympic bout.

Sweden's Fredrik Loof and Max Salminen (far left) won the Star class Sailing at the expense of Great Britain's Iain Percy and Andrew Simpson

Great Britain's Andy Murray jumps for joy after claiming the men's Tennis Singles title with an emphatic win over Roger Federer of Switzerland in the gold medal match on Wimbledon's Centre Court. Murray later added a silver medal alongside Laura Robson in the Mixed Doubles

**Above:** Olga Rypakova earned another gold medal for Kazakhstan in the women's Triple Jump

**Left:** Iran's Hamid Soryan (in red) won the first Greco-Roman Wrestling gold medal of the Games when he overcame Rovshan Bayramov of Azerbaijan

**Below left:** Sanya Richards-Ross of the USA won the women's 400m while Great Britain's Christine Ohuruogu (second from bottom) took the silver medal

**Above right:** Chinese gymnast Kai Zou won gold in the men's Floor Competition

**Below right:** China earned their fifth Diving gold of the Games as Minxia Wu won the women's 3m Springboard

**Below:** Great Britain gymnast Louis Smith had to settle for silver in the Pommel Horse Competition despite finishing level with Krisztian Berki of Hungary, who won on a tie-break

# For the record

## World records
**Weightlifting – women's +75kg**
Lulu Zhou (China) 333kg

## Olympic records
**Athletics – women's Marathon**
Tiki Gelana (Ethiopia) 2:23.07

**Athletics – men's 100m**
Usain Bolt (Jamaica) 9.63

> **'I have lost some tough matches. I've had a lot of questions asked about me many times. I'm just glad that today I managed to put on a performance '**
>
> *Great Britain's Andy Murray reflecting on winning the men's Tennis Singles*

## Team GB moment of the day
Ben Ainslie started his Olympic journey by winning a silver medal in the Laser class as a 19-year-old at Atlanta 1996 and at his home Games, 16 years on, he took his place as the greatest sailor in Olympic history by winning his fourth successive gold medal. His victory in the Finn class at Weymouth and Portland saw Ainslie beat the medal record of Danish sailor Paul Elvstrom and was a further demonstration of the British sailors longevity at the top of his sport.

Once more he did it in spectacular fashion, lying second going into the medal race which effectively meant he had to beat the leader, Denmark's Jonas Hogh-Christensen, to take the gold. He did exactly that and said afterwards: 'I don't think that will ever settle in. That race was certainly one of the most nerve-racking experiences of my life but thankfully I came through."

## Golden Games moment
Having promised to 'blow people's minds' at London 2012, Usain Bolt came good on his pledge with a performance that sent the Olympic Stadium into meltdown on Day 9. The 25-year-old confirmed his position as the fastest man on the planet with a stunning performance to win the 100m gold medal in 9.63 to the delight of the 80,000 people who were lucky enough to be present to witness another golden moment in Olympic history. The roar of the crowd could be heard all across the Olympic Park as the Jamaican star crossed the line in a new Olympic record to retain the title he had won at Beijing four years earlier.

By recording yet another awe-inspiring victory, Bolt also silenced the critics who had suggested the air of invincibility had left the sprinting superstar after losing to team-mate Yohan Blake in the Jamaican trials for London 2012. Unlike four years earlier, when his celebrations started even before the finish of the race, Bolt saved his showboating for after the gold was in the bag, delighting on-lookers with his trademark flamboyant celebrations on his lap of honour alongside silver medallist Blake. ■

# Day 10

## Monday, 6 August 2012

## Going for gold

**Athletics**
Women's Pole Vault • Women's Shot Put • Men's 400m
Hurdles • Women's 3000m Steeplechase • Men's 400m

**Cycling – Track**
Men's Sprint

**Equestrian**
Jumping Team Competition

**Gymnastics**
Men's Rings Competition • Women's Uneven Bars
Competition • Men's Vault Competition

**Sailing**
Men's Laser • Women's Laser Radial

**Shooting**
Men's 50m Rifle 3 Positions • Men's Trap

**Weightlifting**
Men's 105kg

**Wrestling – Greco-Roman**
Men's 60kg • Men's 84kg • Men's 120kg

**Right:** Peter Charles on his horse
Vindicat jumped clear on the final
round of a dramatic jump-off against
the Netherlands to win the Equestrian
Team Jumping, Great Britain's first
Jumping gold medal since Helsinki 1952

# A day of drama

## 6 August 2012

**As London 2012 entered its final full week of competition, the pure sporting theatre across a whole range of sports continued on Day 10 as new Olympic champions both young and old were crowned.**

Many fans were still coming to terms with a spectacular weekend of competition but there was no let-up to the drama on Day 10, with Great Britain's showjumpers among those to take centre stage.

The British team, consisting of Nick Skelton, Ben Maher, Scott Brash and Peter Charles, went into the second day of the Team Competition tied for second with the Netherlands, Switzerland and Sweden, three penalties behind surprise leaders Saudi Arabia. But at the end of a fascinating second round they shared the lead with the Netherlands, which

set up an astonishing finale. The two nations were forced to go head-to-head in a jump-off to decide who would take the Olympic gold medal. It was the Dutch who cracked under the pressure, with Mikael van der Vleuten and Marc Houtzager both knocking fences down, while Maher and Skelton both jumped clear. It was left to Charles to secure gold for Team GB and his faultless ride left the Netherlands with silver, while Saudi Arabia clinched bronze. The victory was the host nation's first Equestrian Jumping gold medal since the Helsinki 1952 Games and the first medal of any description since a Team

Competition silver in Los Angeles 28 years earlier.

While the showjumpers' medal quest went down to the wire at Greenwich Park, Jason Kenny justified his selection for the men's Track Cycling Sprint event by convincingly taking gold with victory over French powerhouse Gregory Bauge at the Velodrome. The 24-year-old from Bolton was chosen over reigning Olympic champion Chris Hoy, following the decision to allow only one rider from each nation to compete in each event, and disposed of Trinidad and Tobago's Njisane Phillip in the semi-finals. Though a closely-fought final against Bauge was predicted, Kenny hadn't quite read the script and comfortably out-cycled his opponent to secure gold in two rounds. The medal marked Kenny's first Olympic gold as an individual competitor, having previously won two as a member of the men's Team Sprint competition.

The day's medal action had started earlier in the afternoon on the waters of Weymouth and Portland, where another two events reached their climax. Australia's Tom Slingsby put a disappointing performance at Beijing 2008 behind him to take gold in the men's One-Person Dinghy (Laser). Having been favourite going into the

The victorious British Equestrian Team Jumping quartet, from left, Nick Skelton, Ben Maher, Scott Brash and Peter Charles

> **' We lost it, we won it, we lost it and then finally we won it back. Without this crowd we could never have done it '**
>
> *Nick Skelton after Great Britain won Equestrian Team Jumping gold in a jump-off*

**Above:** Beth Tweddle's bronze in the Uneven Bars Competition was the very first individual Olympic Games Gymnastics medal ever won by a British woman

**Right:** Russian athlete Yuliya Zaripova leads out of the water jump on her way to victory in the women's 3000m Steeplechase

**Below right:** At the age of 19, Kirani James added the Olympic men's 400m title to his world championship and earned Grenada their first ever Olympic gold medal

**Below:** Veteran athlete Felix Sanchez was in floods of tears during the Victory Ceremony after winning his second men's 400m Hurdles title at the age of 34

Games four years ago, Slingsby performed well below expectations to finish a lowly 22nd. The 27-year-old made amends for that setback by seeing off the threat of Pavlos Kontides, whose silver was Cyprus' first medal in Olympic history, and the Australian celebrated victory so wildly he tipped his boat over. The women's Laser Radial saw Lijia Xu of China crowned champion and, despite having an impressive week and heading into the final race with every chance of claiming a medal, Ireland's Olympic debutant Annalise Murphy narrowly missed out on her chance to take the country's first medal of London 2012 as she finished fourth.

Day 10 saw the curtain come down on the Shooting events at The Royal Artillery Barracks, but spectators were in for an explosive conclusion. Having qualified for the men's Trap final with the lowest score, Croatia's Giovanni Cernogoraz made a surprising surge to the top of the leaderboard by missing only once while his opponents faltered. The 29-year-old ended up in a shoot-off for gold with world champion Massimo Fabbrizi, and it was the Italian who missed first to give Cernogoraz the unexpected gold medal. Italy's Niccolo Campriani took gold in the day's other Shooting event

– the men's 50m Rifle 3 Positions – comfortably fending off the challenge of the Republic of Korea's Jonghyun Kim and Matt Emmons of the United States, who took silver and bronze.

British Gymnastics' leading lady Beth Tweddle made history at the North Greenwich Arena by becoming the first woman to win an individual Olympic medal in the sport for Great Britain, achieving third place in the women's Uneven Bars Competition. Russia's Aliya Mustafina claimed gold, while Kexin He of China took silver.

## Last-gasp success

The men's Rings Competition final saw a dramatic finale as Brazil's Arthur Nabarrete Zanetti took a last-gasp victory. Defending champion Yibing Chen of China looked set to retain his Olympic title and led the way throughout the competition after he competed first, scoring an impressive 15.800. However, Zanetti was the last man to go and snatched gold with a score of 15.900, with Italy's Matteo Morandi finishing in the bronze medal position. In the final Artistic Gymnastics event of the day, Hak Seon Yang of the Republic of Korea took gold in the men's Vault Competition.

On a busy day at London's ExCeL, there were gold medals for Iran's Omid Noroozi, Alan Khugaev of Russia and Cuban Mijain Lopez in the 60kg, 84kg and 120kg Greco-Roman Wrestling events respectively, while Ukraine's Oleksiy Torokhtiy was crowned champion in the men's 105kg Weightlifting.

The Olympic Stadium once again provided the setting for the evening's primetime entertainment, with five gold medals up for grabs. At the age of 34, Felix Sanchez of the Dominican Republic stormed to a remarkable victory in the men's 400m Hurdles, eight years after winning gold in the event at Athens 2004 and posting exactly the same time of 47.63. The achievement was made even more outstanding by the fact he defeated an illustrious field that included favourite Javier Culson, world champion Dai Greene and reigning Olympic champion Angelo Taylor to take gold. Russia's Yuliya Zaripova was crowned victor in the women's 3000m Steeplechase, before 19-year-old Kirani James won Grenada's first ever Olympic gold medal with victory in the men's 400m, finishing ahead of Luguelin Santos – who capped a successful night of Athletics for the Dominican Republic. In the field events, Nadzeya Ostapchuk of Belarus won the women's Shot Put, but later failed a doping control test and so the gold medal was awarded to defending champion Valerie Adams of New Zealand. Jennifer Suhr of the USA was crowned champion in the women's Pole Vault.

Elsewhere, Great Britain's men's Basketball team recorded their first Olympic victory since 1948, defeating China 90-58 to climb off the bottom of their group, while Team GB's Nicola Adams and Katie Taylor of Ireland were among those to guarantee themselves a medal in the women's Boxing competition by qualifying for the semi-finals.

New Zealand's Valerie Adams threw 20.70m in the women's Shot Put to retain her Olympic title

Jason Kenny
secured his third
Olympic title but
his first individual
gold after beating
three-time world
champion Gregory
Bauge in the
men's Sprint

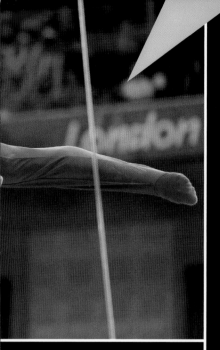

**Above:** Brazil's Arthur Nabarrete Zanetti won a last-gasp Gymnastics gold medal in the Rings Competition

**Far left:** USA athlete Jennifer Suhr beat the likes of double Olympic champion Elena Isinbaeva to win the women's Pole Vault

**Left:** Drew Sullivan soars towards the basket as Great Britain broke their men's Basketball duck against China

**Below:** Tom Slingsby put aside his poor finish at Beijing 2008 to win gold for Australia in the Laser event

# For the record

## World records

**Canoe Sprint – women's Kayak Four (K4) 500m**
Poland 1:30.338

**Shooting – men's Trap qualifying**
Michael Diamond (Australia) 125

## Olympic records

**Shooting – men's 50m Rifle 3 Positions**
Niccolo Campriani (Italy) 1278.5

**Shooting – men's Trap**
Massimo Fabbrizi (Italy) and Giovanni Cernogoraz (Croatia) 146

' **Before we went up for the very last ride it dawned on me that if Chris was in my shoes here, there was no way he'd lose this one** '

*Track Cycling gold medallist Jason Kenny on the pressure of being chosen for the men's Sprint ahead of Great Britain team-mate Chris Hoy*

## Team GB moment of the day

Having entered the second day of competition in joint second place in the Equestrian Team Jumping, Great Britain's riders had every reason to feel confident of a medal, but the fashion in which they galloped to gold had spectators on the edge of their seats. As overnight leaders Saudi Arabia fell away, the British team of Nick Skelton, Ben Maher, Scott Brash and Peter Charles found themselves tied with the Netherlands, forcing a jump-off for gold – the Equestrian equivalent of a penalty shoot-out.

As Dutch riders cracked, it was left to Charles to complete the decisive attempt and the Liverpool-born rider put in a faultless performance to secure gold for the host nation in front of a 23,000-strong crowd at Greenwich Park. Charles' team-mate, 54-year-old Skelton – participating in his sixth Games – had recovered from hip replacement surgery in 2011 to inspire his team to gold with three clear rounds out of three across the whole competition. The victory ensured a first British Olympic Jumping title since 1952.

## Golden Games Moment

The Dominican Republic's Felix Sanchez's best years appeared to be behind him when the 2004 Olympic 400m Hurdles champion failed to qualify from the heats in Beijing four years later. However, the New York-born star made a remarkable return to form for London 2012 and, on Day 10, claimed a stunning gold to become the event's oldest ever medallist at 34 years and 342 days – breaking a record that had stood for 104 years.

Sanchez, who ran with a picture of his deceased grandmother hidden behind the pinned name on his vest, defeated a field full of star names and amazingly recorded the same time as he did for his Athens 2004 victory (47.63). Sanchez's Victory Ceremony ended up producing one of the iconic images of the Games as the athlete sobbed his way through his national anthem, winning a place in the hearts of the capacity crowd at the Olympic Stadium who applauded and roared in support of the champion's show of emotion. ∎

# Day 11

Tuesday, 7 August 2012

## Going for gold

**Athletics**
Men's High Jump • Men's Discus Throw • Women's 100m Hurdles • Men's 1500m

**Cycling – Track**
Women's Omnium • Women's Sprint • Men's Keirin

**Diving**
Men's 3m Springboard

**Equestrian**
Dressage Team Competition

**Gymnastics**
Men's Parallel Bars Competition • Women's Balance Beam Competition • Men's Horizontal Bar Competition • Women's Floor Competition

**Sailing**
Men's Windsurfer (RS:X) • Women's Windsurfer (RS:X)

**Synchronised Swimming**
Women's Duets

**Table Tennis**
Women's Team

**Triathlon**
Men's Triathlon

**Weightlifting**
Men's +105kg

**Wrestling**
Men's Greco-Roman 66kg • Men's Greco-Roman 96kg

**Right:** Cyclist Chris Hoy bowed out of Olympic Games competition by winning the men's Keirin and collecting a British record sixth Olympic gold medal of his career

# Records tumble

**As the medal tally kept on climbing, Great Britain had not had it so good for more than a century and, on Day 11 of London 2012, Chris Hoy took the headlines as the host nation continued to exceed expectations.**

Five days of competition still remained but already this was the most successful Olympic Games for Great Britain since London first hosted the sporting showpiece in 1908, with Chris Hoy leading the way with an historic sixth career gold to help take Team GB past the total of 47 medals won at Beijing 2008.

Having claimed gold in the men's Team Sprint on the opening night in the Velodrome, Hoy brought the curtain down on the scintillating Track Cycling programme by retaining his men's Keirin title, making him the most successful Briton in Olympic history. In the early stages of the final, Hoy was third behind the motorised Derny and appeared boxed in as Awang Azizulhasni of Malaysia made his move just before the pace-setting bike left the track. However, the Scot swiftly found a gap and eased to the front of the six-man group before turning on the power in the final lap to set up a close battle for the line with Germany's Maximillian Levy. The 36-year-old maintained his momentum into the final bend to triumph on the Olympic stage once more, joining fellow cyclist Bradley Wiggins on a record seven career Olympic medals. As had been the case throughout the week, Great Britain dominated the medal action at the Olympic Park venue. The evening kicked off with Laura Trott adding victory in the women's Omnium to the women's Team Pursuit title she captured earlier in the week. The 20-year-old, who took up cycling aged eight to help regulate her breathing after being born with a collapsed lung, was two points behind the United States' Sarah Hammer entering the final discipline – the 500m Time Trial – but claimed her third win from six disciplines to overhaul the deficit and win by a point. There was disappointment, however, for Victoria Pendleton, who was denied a golden departure from Track Cycling by an inspired performance from Australia's Anna Meares in the women's Sprint, who defeated the Briton in two rounds.

The day's gold-medal action had started in London's Hyde Park, where the podium turned out to be a real family affair for the Brownlee brothers – Alistair and Jonathan – who took gold and bronze respectively. After swimming 1.5km in The Serpentine and negotiating a 43km course on their bikes, the triathletes endured

Chris Hoy was unable to hold back the tears as he prepared to stand on the top step of the podium for the final time

> **We made no secret that we wanted to get both of us on the podium – that's not an easy thing to do considering Britain's never won a medal in Triathlon**
>
> *Men's Triathlon champion Alistair Brownlee on making the podium with bronze medallist brother Jonathan*

**Above:** British riders Carl Hester, Laura Bechtolsheimer and Charlotte Dujardin take a lap of honour in Greenwich Park after winning the Dressage Team Competition

**Right:** Great Britain's Brownlee brothers, Alistair (30) and Jonathan (31), dive into The Serpentine in Hyde Park at the start of the Triathlon

**Below:** Sally Pearson (third left) is out in front as she heads for victory in the women's 100m Hurdles, setting an Olympic record as she wins Australia's first Athletics gold of London 2012

a gruelling 10km run, which saw Alistair Brownlee recording a time that was just a minute and a half slower than Mo Farah's 10,000m-winning performance. The new Olympic champion even had enough time to pick up a Union Jack and walk across the finish line to become Britain's first ever medallist in the event, fending off competition from Spain's Javier Gomez and brother Jonathan, who finished third despite incurring a 15-second penalty for getting on his bike too early in the transition zone.

At Greenwich Park, Great Britain's riders made history by claiming the nation's first Olympic Dressage medal, riding away with gold in the Team Competition 24 hours after their Jumping counterparts achieved the same feat. Following a closely-fought contest, the team of Carl Hester, Laura Bechtolsheimer and Charlotte Dujardin held off rivals Germany and the Netherlands to take the title. The victory far surpassed the nation's previous best performance at the Games, a sixth-place finish in Beijing four years earlier.

In Weymouth and Portland, Dorian van Rijsselberge of the Netherlands was the convincing winner of the men's Windsurfer (RS:X) title, while Great Britain's Nick Dempsey took silver to make up for finishing fourth in Beijing. It was a day of firsts in the women's competition as Maria Alabau won Spain's first gold of the Games ahead of Finland's Tuuli Petaja, who won her country's first medal of any description at London 2012.

## Gymnastics climax

The afternoon saw the final day of Artistic Gymnastics take place at the North Greenwich Arena, where four gold medals were up for grabs. The day was dominated by China, who took gold in both the men's Parallel Bars Competition and the women's Balance Beam Competition with victories for Zhe Feng and Linlin Deng respectively, while Alexandra Raisman of the United States took gold in the women's Floor Competition and the Netherlands' Epke Zonderland was crowned champion in the men's Horizontal Bars Competition.

China took another step towards winning all the Table Tennis gold medals with victory in the women's Team Competition, while Russia continued to dominate the world of Synchronised Swimming by taking a fourth consecutive Olympic title in the women's Duets. At ExCeL, Hyeonwoo Kim made history as he became the Republic of Korea's first ever gold medallist in the 66kg division of men's Greco-Roman Wrestling, while Iran won their third gold in as many days as Ghasem Rezaei beat Russia's Rustam Totrov in the 96kg category.

The success did not end there for Iran, as Behdad Salimikordasiabi took gold in a meeting of the world's strongest men in the +105kg Weightlifting, in an event where reigning champion Matthias Steiner of Germany was forced to withdraw after dropping the bar on his head and shoulder during his second attempt in the snatch.

Russia's Ilya Zakharov ended China's bid for a clean sweep of the gold medals in the Diving with victory in the men's 3m Springboard. The event threw up one of the Games' more heart-warming stories as Great Britain's Chris Mears, who required life-saving surgery on a ruptured spleen during a youth diving competition in 2009, was one of only two competitors to achieve a score of over 100 points for a single dive in the final, where he finished ninth despite being ranked 48th in the world.

In the evening's action at the Olympic Stadium, Russia's Ivan Ukhov got the ball rolling with gold in the men's High Jump, where Robbie Grabarz claimed bronze to take Team GB's medal tally to 48 – one more than Beijing 2008. Australia's Sally Pearson lived up to her billing as the favourite in the women's 100m Hurdles as she won gold in Olympic record time, before Robert Harting of Germany was crowned champion in the men's Discus Throw and Algeria's Taoufik Makhloufi took the men's 1500m title with a dominant display.

Taoufik Makhloufi of Algeria celebrates as he approaches the line to win the men's 1500m

Alistair Brownlee was able to slow down and collect a Union Jack as he headed for the finishing line after a commanding performance in the men's Triathlon

**Above left:** Natalia Ishchenko and Svetlana Romashina won the Synchronised Swimming Duets gold medal for Russia in the Aquatics Centre

**Left:** Ning Ding, Yue Guo and Xiaoxia Li celebrate China's gold medal in the women's Table Tennis Team Competition after beating Japan in the final

**Below left:** Robert Harting of Germany celebrates winning the men's Discus Throw by trying his hand at the hurdles laid out in the Olympic Stadium

**Above right:** Laura Trott of Great Britain earned her second gold medal of the Games when she won the Omnium

**Right:** Dorian van Rijsselberge of the Netherlands (right) won the men's Windsurfer (RS:X) gold medal. Great Britain's Nick Dempsey (left) won silver

**Below right:** Gold medallist Behdad Salimikordasiabi of Iran celebrates with fans after winning the men's +105kg Weightlifting

# For the record

## Olympic records
**Athletics – women's 100m Hurdles**
Sally Pearson (Australia) 12.35

' **People see the finished product, they see the gold medals. They don't realise just how hard it is. All these days you've doubted it, been injured, ill, your form hasn't been there, races you've lost. The way the British team has performed here it almost looks like it's easy. It's anything but. It's the pinnacle of everything you've worked for and you realise that's your little mark in history** '

*Chris Hoy after winning the sixth Olympic gold medal of his career*

## Team GB moment of the day

Chris Hoy's place in British sporting history was never in doubt, but on Day 11 of London 2012 he cemented his place as the country's most successful Olympian by winning his sixth gold medal. After leaving it late to make his final push for the finish, Hoy was initially unsure whether he had won the Keirin Track Cycling title at the Velodrome. 'I shut my eyes when I lunged,' he said. 'I didn't want to look. I drove all the way to the line, threw the bike and I heard this massive roar and realised it was for me. It's the most incredible feeling when you finally cross the line and you realise you've won.'

After being greeted with a guard of honour by members of his team, Hoy climbed to the top step of the podium for a sixth and probably final time at an Olympic Games, surpassing Sir Steve Redgrave's record, and struggled to hold back the tears as the National Anthem played.

## Golden Games moment

Russia have dominated the world of Olympic Synchronised Swimming since Sydney 2000 and continued to set the standard with a spectacular victory in the women's Duets on Day 11. Having won gold four years earlier in the women's Teams event, Natalia Ishchenko and Svetlana Romashina decided to go it alone for London 2012 and amazed the judges by performing a haunting routine inspired by horror films *Surprisia* and *Sleepy Hollow*.

The performance earned them a staggering score of 98.900 – just 1.100 off perceived perfection – which, when added to their technical score, gave them a combined total of 197.100 out of a maximum 200. The duo, who have both had illustrious careers, joined an exclusive club of athletes – all Russian – who have won Olympic gold in both the Teams and Duets events and secured their country's seventh consecutive Olympic gold in the sport. ■

' **It is amazing that I learned to balance and ride on a bareback donkey** '

*Great Britain Dressage gold medallist Carl Hester on his humble beginnings on the Channel Island of Sark*

# Day 12

## Wednesday, 8 August 2012

## Going for gold

**Athletics**
Women's Long Jump • Women's 400m Hurdles •
Women's 200m • Men's 110m Hurdles

**Beach Volleyball**
Women's Beach Volleyball

**Canoe Sprint**
Men's Kayak Single (K1) 1000m • Men's Canoe Single
(C1) 1000m • Men's Kayak Double (K2) 1000m •
Women's Kayak Four (K4) 500m

**Equestrian**
Jumping Individual Competition

**Sailing**
Men's Skiff (49er)

**Table Tennis**
Men's Team

**Taekwondo**
Women's Under 49kg • Men's Under 58kg

**Wrestling**
Women's Freestyle 48kg • Women's Freestyle 63kg

**Right:** Misty May-Treanor marked her
retirement from the sport by winning
a third successive Olympic gold medal
in the women's Beach Volleyball with
United States team-mate Kerri Walsh

# Shining stars

**The United States dominated the podium at both Horse Guards Parade and the Olympic Stadium on a scintillating day of action, while Hungary, China and Japan were among the other nations with much to celebrate.**

Much of Day 12's medal action took place after dark and, as the floodlights shone down on London's venues, the athletes competing inside were hoping to make it a night to remember.

The Stars and Stripes were out in force at Horse Guards Parade as the United States' Misty May-Treanor and Kerri Walsh took on compatriots April Ross and Jennifer Kessy for Beach Volleyball gold and national bragging rights. The popular central London tourist site, which is a stone's throw away from Downing Street, had proved to be one of the most vibrant locations during London 2012, generating atmospheres more akin to the host nation's football terraces than those normally seen at Beach Volleyball arenas. The spectators who packed into the cauldron-like venue were treated to a masterclass from two-time Olympic champions May-Treanor and Walsh, who added a third gold medal to their impressive haul. The pair made short work of their opponents, claiming gold in under 40 minutes with a 21-16 21-16 victory. The win was made all the more remarkable by the fact Walsh took a break from the sport after Beijing 2008 to start a family – giving birth to two sons – and only made her return to major events in 2011. With May-Treanor planning to retire for good after London 2012, the final marked the last outing for the pair, who have never lost an Olympic match together and have only ever conceded one set at all the Olympic Games.

There was further success for the United States at the Olympic Stadium, where they dominated the night's Athletics programme. Allyson Felix set the standard in the women's 200m as she led from the start to clinch gold in a time of 21.88 and fend off a field that included reigning 100m world champion and USA team-mate Carmelita Jeter, who took bronze, and 2008 Olympic champion Veronica Campbell-Brown. Fellow United States athlete Aries Merritt followed up Felix's gold medal-winning performance by storming to victory in the men's 110m Hurdles ahead of compatriot

Aries Merritt edged out team-mate Jason Richardson as the United States won gold and silver in the men's 110m Hurdles

> ❝It's just awesome, I've wanted it for so long. This moment is really priceless. I am so overjoyed❞
>
> *United States athlete Allyson Felix after winning the women's 200m final*

**Above:** Australian gold medallists Nathan Outteridge and Iain Jensen lead British pair Stevie Morrison and Ben Rhodes in the final 49er race

**Right:** Allyson Felix began a golden night for the United States on the track at the Olympic Stadium as she won the women's 200m final

**Below:** Argentina players celebrate after beating Great Britain 2-1 in the semi-final to reach the gold medal match of the women's Hockey

Jason Richardson. A glorious night for the United States was rounded off by Brittney Reese, who leapt to gold in the women's Long Jump and was joined on the podium by third-placed team-mate Janay Deloach. Russia's Natalya Antyukh was the night's other Athletics gold medallist with victory in the women's 400m Hurdles, while Lashinda Demus took silver for the USA.

As the women's Freestyle Wrestling events got under way, it was Japan's night as they took both of the golds on offer. The first came in the 48kg division for Hitomi Obara, before Kaori Icho continued her domination of the 63kg category by taking her third consecutive Olympic title to extend her remarkable winning streak to 153 fights. On Taekwondo's opening night, China's Jingyu Wu successfully defended her Under 49kg Olympic title after beating veteran Spaniard Brigitte Yague Enrique, before Spain went one better in the men's Under 58kg category thanks to Joel Gonzalez Bonilla's victory over the Republic of Korea's Daehoon Lee in the final.

In the day's earlier events, there was double delight for Hungary as the first Canoe Sprint medals were handed out on the lake at Eton Dorney. Rudolf Dombi and Roland Kokeny were crowned champions in the men's Kayak Double (K2) 1000m, before the women's Kayak Four (K4) 500m crew took Hungary to a tally of six London 2012 gold medals – double what they achieved in Beijing four years earlier. Norway's Eirik Veras Larsen made a late surge in the men's Kayak Single (K1) 1000m to take gold ahead of Canada's Adam van Koeverden and Max Hoff of Germany, while Hoff's compatriot Sebastian Brendel emerged victorious in the men's Canoe Single (C1) 1000m.

## Delight down under

With Australia and New Zealand having already confirmed their places on the top two steps of the podium with gold and silver respectively, the final race of the men's 49er served as a lap of honour for the two neighbouring nations. Great Britain were among the countries battling for bronze but, after losing ground on their rivals on the second upwind leg, Stevie Morrison and Ben Rhodes struggled to fight back and eventually lost out to the Danish pairing of Allan Norregaard and Peter Lang, who took the last available space on the podium.

Day 12 at Greenwich Park witnessed Switzerland's Steve Guerdat win gold in the Equestrian Jumping Individual Competition. The 30-year-old was the only rider to perform two clear rounds in the final, while the quest for silver went down to a dramatic jump-off between Gerco Schroder of the Netherlands and Ireland's Cian O'Connor. The Irishman, riding Blue Loyd 12, gave it everything to clock a faster time than Schroder in the jump-off but his Dutch rival, whose horse was aptly called London, gave a strong enough performance to secure his second silver of the Games.

Over at ExCeL, China capped an impressive week and a half in the Table Tennis with victory in the men's Team competition to complete a clean sweep of gold medals for the second successive Games. The team, consisting of Long Ma, Jike Zhang and Hao Wang, took their country's medal tally in the sport to four golds and two silvers as they comprehensively disposed of their opponents from the Republic of Korea, beating them 3-0. The victory followed up the Team success of China's women 24 hours earlier as well as the Individual golds claimed by Zhang and Xiaoxia Li.

It was a dramatic day elsewhere as the Games' team competitions neared their golden climax. In the Handball quarter-finals, Hungary needed two sessions of extra time to get past 2008 silver medallists Iceland, who were on the verge of going through in normal time before having a penalty acrobatically saved with just 15 seconds remaining. Hungary raced to the other end of the court to level the score at 27-27 and force the additional time. There were further dramatic scenes at the Riverbank Arena, where the Netherlands required penalties against New Zealand to reach the final of the women's Hockey after the match ended 2-2, while Great Britain fell to a 2-1 defeat at the hands of Argentina.

Rudolf Dombi and Roland Kokeny began a Hungarian double in the Canoe Sprint when they won the K2 final

Brittney Reese won the United States' third Athletics gold medal of the evening when she soared to victory in the women's Long Jump

**Above:** Kaori Icho of Japan won a third Olympic gold when she beat Ruixue Jing of China in the women's 63kg Freestyle Wrestling

**Below:** Mate Lekai shoots during Hungary's thrilling Handball 34-33 quarter-final win over Iceland

**Right:** The United States' domination on the Olympic Stadium track on the evening of Day 12 was broken when Russia's Natalya Antyukh narrowly won the women's 400m Hurdles gold medal from Lashinda Demus, who took the silver medal for the USA

**Far right top:** Nicola Adams (in blue) beat India's Mary Kom to reach the women's Boxing Fly Weight (51kg) final

**Far right bottom:** Cian O'Connor of Ireland on his way to bronze in the Equestrian Jumping Individual Competition

## Team GB moment of the day

Nicola Adams was left just one more win away from realising her 17-year-old dream of hanging an Olympic gold medal around her neck after cruising through her women's Fly Weight (51kg) semi-final against India's Mary Kom. The 29-year-old boxed superbly amid another raucous ExCeL atmosphere to repel the relentless advances of the smaller Kom and book a gold medal match against China's world number one, Ren Cancan.

It was testament to Adams' quality that she made a bout against the ferocious Kom look relatively easy. Kom is a five-time world champion but had to step up two weights to reach the Games, and the size difference was the key

❝ **I've been training for this moment since I was 12 years old and to think it is finally here is just incredible. I am going to treat it like a normal tournament and hopefully the crowd will give me a boost to edge away and get the gold. I've beaten her once before and I'm definitely confident I can go out and do it again** ❞

*Great Britain boxer Nicola Adams*

## Golden Games moment

The old saying that 'if at first you don't succeed, try, try again' certainly proved to be wise words in the case of Japanese wrestler Hitomi Obara. After failing to make her country's team for Athens 2004, and refusing to battle with her sister for a place in the 2008 squad, the 30-year-old retired from the sport twice but decided to give it another go ahead of London 2012 and successfully made the cut.

Obara justified her selection with a remarkable march to gold in the women's Freestyle 48kg, recovering from a 4-0 defeat in the first period to take the next two 1-0 and 2-0 to beat Azerbaijan's Mariya Stadnyk to the top of the podium. It was a successful night for Japan on the Wrestling mat as Kaori Icho became the first woman to win three wrestling golds at the Olympic Games, with victory in the women's Freestyle 63kg.

*It means the world. We set our expectations really high as a team, as people and as players. We want this game to grow and we set the bar very high and we extended that bar and set it even higher*

*Women's Beach Volleyball gold medallist Misty May-Treanor*

# Day 13

## Going for gold

### Athletics
Men's Triple Jump • Men's 800m • Men's 200m •
Women's Javelin Throw • Men's Decathlon

### Beach Volleyball
Men's Beach Volleyball

### Boxing
Women's Fly Weight (48-51kg) • Women's Light Weight
(57-60kg) • Women's Middle Weight (69-75kg)

### Canoe Sprint
Men's Canoe Double (C2) 1000m • Men's Kayak Four
(K4) 1000m • Women's Kayak Single (K1) 500m •
Women's Kayak Double (K2) 500m

### Diving
Women's 10m Platform

### Equestrian
Dressage Individual Competition

### Football
Women's Football

### Swimming
Women's 10km Marathon Swim

### Taekwondo
Women's -57kg • Men's -68kg

### Water Polo
Women's Water Polo

### Wrestling
Women's Freestyle 72kg • Women's Freestyle 55kg

**Right:** Usain Bolt is flanked by
silver medallist Yohan Blake (right)

# Legends are made

## 9 August 2012

**Day 13 proved to be a momentous day in Olympic history as Usain Bolt once again completed a sprint double, a world record was broken on the track and the first ever gold medals were handed out in women's Boxing.**

London 2012 has provided some memorable moments to add to the Olympic Games' long and illustrious history and there were even more to come on the Athletics track and in the Boxing ring on Day 13.

Having defied his doubters to defend the men's 100m title just five days earlier, Jamaican star Usain Bolt confirmed his status as the king of sprints by becoming the first man to retain an Olympic 200m gold medal. After treating the crowd to a regal wave before the race, the Trelawny-born athlete burst out of the blocks and led throughout as he sprinted his way to sporting royalty – recording a time of 19.32 to take gold ahead of Yohan Blake and Warren Weir, who completed an all-Jamaican podium. Bolt embarked on a lap of honour, celebrating in his usual exuberant style and, as the cameras of the capacity crowd pointed in his direction, the five-time Olympic gold medallist even took time to take some pictures of his own before kissing the finish line and striking his customary pose.

Bolt's was one of a number of outstanding performances on a thrilling night of action at the Olympic Stadium. Kenya's David Rudisha produced a memorable moment of his own, delivering the performance of a lifetime to take gold in the men's 800m in world-record time. The 23-year-old made his intentions clear from the starting gun as he built an early lead, leaving his opponents unable to keep up with the pace. He crossed the line in a breathtaking 1:40.91, finishing ahead of Botswana's Nijel Amos and fellow Kenyan Timothy Kitum, who took silver and bronze respectively.

After a dominant night at the same venue 24 hours earlier, the United States' athletes continued to produce a series of stunning performances. Christian Taylor added Olympic Triple Jump gold to the world title he won in 2011 with a jump of 17.81, while Ashton Eaton triumphed in the men's Decathlon, clocking a new world record for the competition of 10.35 in the 100m. The final Athletics gold of the day went to Barbora Spotakova of the Czech Republic, who took victory in the women's Javelin Throw.

It was a historic day for the Olympic Games as the first ever medals were handed out in women's Boxing. First to step onto the podium's top step was Great Britain's Nicola Adams, who was a 16-7 winner in the Fly Weight final against China's Cancan Ren, much to the delight of

Eventual winner Ashton Eaton (left) leads the 110m hurdles element of the men's Decathlon

‘ **It was hard. I really dedicated myself to my work, I know what London meant to me. I came here and I gave it my all and I'm proud of myself** ’

*Usain Bolt after adding the men's 200m title to his 100m gold medal for the second successive Games*

**Above:** Great Britain's Charlotte Dujardin won the Dressage Individual Competition on her horse Valegro

**Below:** Nicola Adams knocks down China's Cancan Ren on her way to winning the women's Boxing Fly Weight (51kg) final

**Right:** Kenya's David Rudisha set a new world record of 1:40.91 in the men's 800m final

**Bottom:** The 18 members of the United States women's Football squad on the podium after beating Japan 2-1 in the final

a fanatical crowd at London's ExCeL, who rose to their feet in appreciation of the new Olympic champion. The 29-year-old from Leeds floored Ren in the second round on her way to a stunningly comprehensive victory against an opponent who had beaten her in each of the previous two World Championship finals. There was no let-up in the electric atmosphere as Ireland's Katie Taylor then entered the ring to battle for Boxing Light Weight (60kg) gold. The 26-year-old had been roared on throughout the competition by the scores of Irish fans and the Irish flagbearer did not let her compatriots down as she emerged with the Olympic title after a narrow victory over Sofya Ochigava of Russia. In the last of the day's Boxing finals, Claressa Shields of the United States was crowned Olympic champion in the women's Middle Weight (75kg) division.

Day 13 proved to be lucky for Team GB as their impressive tally of gold medals kept on growing. Greenwich Park continued to be a happy hunting ground for the host nation's Equestrian squad as Charlotte Dujardin wowed the judges with a patriotic routine in the Dressage Individual Competition to take gold. The Enfield-born rider and her horse Valegro performed a routine to the tune of *Land of Hope and Glory* and the chimes of Big Ben among others. Joining her on the podium were the Netherlands' Adelinde Cornelissen and fellow Team GB rider Laura Bechtolsheimer.

The host nation also struck gold in Taekwondo, with North Wales' Jade Jones adding her name to the list of Britain's Olympic Champions by embarking on a remarkable journey which resulted in her becoming Great Britain's first ever gold medallist in the sport. The 19-year-old came through a semi-final with world number one Li-Cheng Tseng of Chinese Taipei to meet world champion Hou Yuzhuo of China in the final of the women's

-57kg. The Flint battler was unfazed and emerged with a 10-6 victory from a cagey encounter to secure top spot on the podium. In the men's -68kg, Turkey's Servet Tazegul took gold with a narrow victory over Mohammad Bagheri Motamed of Iran.

## German double

The day's action had once again started on the lake at Eton Dorney, where there were another four Canoe Sprint gold medals to be decided. Germany enjoyed a dominant morning on the water, taking gold in the men's Canoe Double (C2) 1000m and the women's Kayak Double (K2) 500m, while Australia were victorious in the men's Kayak Four (K4) 1000m. In the morning's other race, Danuta Kozak took Hungary's Canoe Sprint gold-medal tally to three with victory in the women's Kayak Single (K1) 500m.

Over in London's Hyde Park, one of the Games' most physically demanding disciplines – the women's Swimming 10km Marathon Swim – attracted another big crowd. Hungary's Eva Risztov led from the start and, as others fell away behind her in the closing stages, she only had to withstand some late pressure

from the United States' Haley Anderson to secure gold, while Great Britain's Keri-Anne Payne finished fourth – agonisingly close to a place on the podium.

In the women's Freestyle Wrestling, Saori Yoshida won her third successive Olympic gold in the 55kg division to maintain Japan's dominance of the event at London 2012, while Russia's Natalia Vorobieva stunned five-time world champion Stanka Zlateva Hristova of Bulgaria to take gold in the women's 72kg. China continued to rule the Diving pool with victory for Ruolin Chen, who defended her title in the women's 10m Platform.

The United States took gold as the women's Water Polo competition reached its conclusion, beating Spain 8-5 in the final, while the USA women's Football team were crowned champions for the third successive time in front of an Olympic record 80,203 fans at Wembley Stadium as they beat Japan 2-1. In one of the night's later events, the German pairing of Julius Brink and Jonas Reckermann defeated top seeds Brazil to take gold as the curtain came down on the men's Beach Volleyball at Horse Guards Parade.

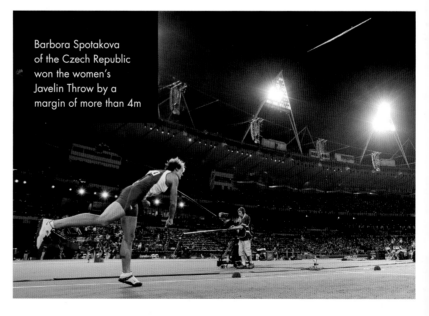

Barbora Spotakova of the Czech Republic won the women's Javelin Throw by a margin of more than 4m

Great Britain's Jade Jones leaps into the arms of coach Paul Green after her victory over world champion Hou Yuzhuo of China in the final of the women's -57kg Taekwondo

**Left:** China continued their domination of the Diving pool when Ruolin Chen won the women's 10m Platform gold

**Above:** Katie Taylor (in red) delighted her throng of Irish fans by winning the women's Boxing Light Weight final

**Right:** Alison Cerutti fails to block Jonas Reckermann's spike during Germany's surprise win over Brazil in the final of the men's Beach Volleyball

**Below left:** The United States team prepares for the women's Water Polo final, in which they beat Spain 8-5

**Below:** The women's 10km Marathon swimmers pass The Serpentine Bridge in Hyde Park

# For the record

*❝ It is a dream come true. I am so happy and overwhelmed with joy right now. I have wanted this all my life and I have done it ❞*

*Great Britain Fly Weight Nicola Adams on winning the first ever women's Boxing gold awarded at the Olympic Games*

## Team GB moment of the day

While Nicola Adams and Charlotte Dujardin were busy putting in stunning performances to claim gold for Team GB, North Wales' Taekwondo teen Jade Jones was on an amazing 12-hour journey to realising her Olympic dreams. Great Britain had never won Olympic gold in the sport and Jones faced an uphill struggle if she hoped to do so on Day 13 of London 2012.

After getting her campaign under way at 10.30am, Jones battled her way through three rounds, including a semi-final encounter with world number one Li-Cheng Tseng of Chinese Taipei, before meeting world champion Hou Yuzhuo in the final at 10.15pm. After a cagey opening two rounds, the Briton went on the offensive and opened up a 5-1 lead heading into the final 30 seconds, before closing out a stunning 6-4 victory. Jones then revealed how the pressure of a home crowd spurred her on to success, saying: 'Before I came out I thought I'm not letting her beat me here in front of the home crowd.'

## Golden Games moment

The roll of honour for the Olympic men's 200m is littered with the names of some of Athletics' all-time greats but on Day 13 of London 2012, one man edged ahead of the rest to become the greatest ever. Jesse Owens, Carl Lewis and Michael Johnson had all experienced the joy of being crowned Olympic champion in the event, but nobody had been able to successfully defend their title.

Having already become only the third man to win two successive 100m gold medals, Jamaica's Usain Bolt rewrote the history books by storming to victory in a second consecutive 200m final .

Despite concerns over his fitness going into the Games, Bolt successfully fended off the challenge of compatriots Yohan Blake and Warren Weir, who took silver and bronze respectively. Upon realising the magnitude of his achievement, Bolt said: 'I've got nothing left to prove. I've showed the world I'm the best and, right now, I just want to enjoy myself. This is my moment. I'll never forget this.' ■

*❝ Rudisha's run will go down in history as one of the greatest Olympic victories ❞*

*Sebastian Coe after David Rudisha won the men's 800m and set a new world record*

# Day 14

## Going for gold

**Athletics**
Men's Pole Vault • Women's Hammer Throw •
Women's 5000m • Women's 4 x 100m Relay •
Women's 1500m • Men's 4 x 400m Relay

**Cycling BMX**
Women's BMX Racing • Men's BMX Racing

**Hockey**
Women's Hockey

**Sailing**
Men's Two-Person Dinghy (470) •
Women's Two-Person Dinghy (470)

**Swimming**
Men's 10km Marathon Swim

**Synchronised Swimming**
Team Competition

**Taekwondo**
Women's Under 67kg • Men's Under 80kg

**Wrestling**
Men's Freestyle 74kg • Men's Freestyle 55kg

**Right:** Carmelita Jeter anchored the United
States quartet to victory in the women's
4 x 100m Relay in a time which broke a
world record that had stood for 27 years

# Sheer brilliance

**The United States women's 4 x 100m Relay team broke a long-standing world record to claim gold on yet another compelling day at London 2012 as medals were won in sports as diverse as Athletics, Sailing and Taekwondo.**

For the second night running, an 80,000-capacity crowd in the Olympic Stadium was lucky enough to witness a stunning world record as the Games continued to deliver exceptional performances.

A day after David Rudisha's wonderful 800m victory, the masterclass produced by the United States in the final of the women's 4 x 100m Relay was nothing short of sensational. The previous world best time of 41.37, set by East Germany, had stood since 1985 but the USA quartet of Tianna Madison, Allyson Felix, Bianca Knight and Carmelita Jeter destroyed the record by clocking 40.82 to dominate the final and claim gold in the event for the first time since Atlanta 1996. The sheer brilliance of the USA team inspired equally superb performances behind them in the battle for the other medals as both Jamaica and Ukraine set new national records to win silver and bronze respectively. The United States' men's 4 x 400m Relay team were unable to match that display as they had to settle for silver behind the Bahamas, with Great Britain just out of the medals in fourth.

In the women's 5000m, Ethiopia's Tirunesh Dibaba was looking to become the first female in Olympic history to win the distance-events double at consecutive Games, having won the 10,000m a week earlier. She led at the bell and battled to hold onto her lead in the home straight but was denied by compatriot Meseret Defar, who sprinted clear to regain the Olympic crown she had won at Athens 2004. Dibaba had to settle for bronze, as Kenya's Vivian Cheruiyot came through to earn silver.

In the night's other track and field action, Turkey celebrated gold and silver in the women's 1500m final as Asli Cakir Alptekin finished ahead of team-mate Gamze Bulut, Russian Federation's Tatyana Lysenko won the women's Hammer Throw in an Olympic record of 78.18 and the men's Pole Vault also saw a new Olympic record achieved as the impressive Frenchman Renaud Lavillenie won with 5.97.

The first medals of the day to be decided were in the Sailing at Weymouth and Portland, where Team GB claimed two silvers. A day earlier, the men's Two-Person Dinghy (470) medal race had to be postponed due to light wind but the top 10 in the class got going at the second time of asking and what unfolded was a fascinating tactical duel between Australia and Great Britain. Team GB's Luke Patience and Stuart Bithell needed at least one boat

Ethiopian Meseret Defar added a second women's 5000m gold medal to the one she won eight years earlier

> ❝ **My coaches told me "this bronze is now your gold medal, so you have to treat it as a final and go for it." That got me in the right state mentally** ❞

*Team GB Taekwondo bronze medallist Lutalo Muhammad*

**Above:** Australia's sailors saw off the challenge of the British crew to win the men's Two-Person Dinghy (470)

**Right:** Dutch joy and Argentinian disappointment after the Netherlands' 2-0 win in the women's Hockey final

**Below:** A new Olympic record gave Tatyana Lysenko victory in the women's Hammer Throw

**Bottom:** Renaud Lavillenie of France clears the bar to win the men's Pole Vault

in between them and the Australian duo of Mathew Belcher and Malcolm Page to claim gold. The British pair got the upper hand early on but then lost ground on their rivals, who finished ahead of the home favourites. There was another chance for the host nation to top the podium in the women's Two-Person Dinghy. Hannah Mills and Saskia Clark were tied at the top of the standings alongside Jo Aleh and Olivia Powrie of New Zealand after the first 10 races of the regatta and were already assured of at least silver, but Aleh and Powrie made a better judgment call on which side of the course to sail on and the Britons could only watch as their rivals powered clear to gold.

In the men's 10km Marathon Swim in The Serpentine in Hyde Park, Tunisia's Oussama Mellouli added to his bronze from the 1500m Freestyle by claiming gold ahead of Germany's Thomas Lurz, who took silver, and bronze medallist Richard Weinberger of Canada. For the second time at London 2012, the Russians proved to be the queens of Synchronised

Swimming by successfully defending their Olympic Team title. Russian Federation saw off China and Spain into silver and bronze respectively, while Team GB impressed in their first ever appearance in the Team Competition at the Games by finishing sixth thanks to their Peter Pan-themed free routine.

## BMX drama
The BMX Cycling came to a close at the BMX Track and, as ever, both the men's and women's finals provided plenty of excitement and drama. At the age of 20, Colombia's Mariana Pajon added Olympic gold to the world title she won in 2011 as she beat Sarah Walker of New Zealand into second. Britain's Shanaze Reade impressed in her three semi-final races but had to settle for sixth in a fiercely-contested final. Her team-mate Liam Phillips fell on the penultimate turn during the men's final – having been well placed up to that point – as Latvia's Maris Strombergs retained the gold medal he won four years earlier after showing

great composure at the front of the field to leave world champion Sam Willoughby of Australia in second.

In the final of the women's Hockey, the Netherlands successfully defended their Olympic title with a 2-0 win over Argentina at the Riverbank Arena. A cagey game was settled midway through the second half as the Dutch scored two penalty corner goals in relatively quick succession. Great Britain's women took the bronze with a 3-1 victory over New Zealand during the afternoon session. There was also a third-place spot on the podium for Britain's Lutalo Muhammad in the Taekwondo -80kg division. The 21-year-old Londoner lost in the quarter-finals, but had a second chance in the repechage and came through to beat Arman Yeremyan of Armenia to secure bronze. Gold in that event went to Sebastian Eduardo Crismanich of Argentina, while the women's -67kg class was won by Kyung Seon Hwang of the Republic of Korea.

In the men's Freestyle Wrestling, Russia's Dzhamal Otarsultanov won the 55kg title, while USA's Jordan Burroughs triumphed in the 74kg division. At the Millennium Stadium, Republic of Korea claimed their first ever Olympic Football medal by beating Japan 2-0 to secure bronze.

In the men's Boxing, Team GB's Luke Campbell and Ireland's John Joe Nevin both won their semi-final bouts in the Bantam Weight (-56kg) division at ExCeL to set up a mouthwatering final. There was further success for the host nation as Fred Evans progressed to fight for gold in the men's Welter Weight (up to 69kg) and Anthony Joshua won his Super Heavy Weight (+91kg) semi-final clash. There was disappointment though for Britain's Anthony Ogogo and Nevin's countrymen Paddy Barnes and Michael Conlan, who all lost in their respective semi-finals and had to settle for bronze.

Asli Cakir Alptekin and Gamze Bulut completed a gold and silver one-two for Turkey in the women's 1500m

There was spectacular action – and plenty of thrills and spills – as the BMX Cycling reached a climax with men's gold for Maris Strombergs of Latvia and victory in the women's final for Colombian world champion Mariana Pajon

**Above:** Russian Federation, who have won the world championship every year since 1998, retained their Olympic gold medal in the Synchronised Swimming Team Competition

**Left:** Great Britain's Lutalo Muhammad won bronze in the Taekwondo -80kg after coming through the repechage

**Top right:** New Zealand pair Jo Aleh and Olivia Powrie got the better of British rivals Hannah Mills and Saskia Clark to win the women's Two-Person Dinghy (470)

**Below:** Oussama Mellouliof Tunisia dominated the men's 10k Marathon Swim, having already won bronze in the Aquatics Centre

**Right:** Ramon Miller keeps Angelo Taylor at bay as Bahamas beat the United States to the gold medal in the men's 4 x 400m Relay

**Below right:** Jordan Burroughs (in red), who won the men's Freestyle Wrestling 74kg gold me in action against bronze medallist Denis Tsargush of Russian Federation

# For the record

## World records
**Athletics – women's 4 x 100m Relay**
United States 40.82

## Olympic records
**Athletics – women's Hammer Throw**
Tatyana Lysenko (Russia) 78.18
**Athletics – men's Pole Vault**
Renaud Lavillenie (France) 5.97
**Canoe Sprint – women's Kayak Single (K1) 200m**
Lisa Carrington (New Zealand) 40.528
**Canoe Sprint – women's Kayak Double (K2) 200m**
Yury Postrigay and Alexander Dyachenko (Russia) 32.051
**Canoe Sprint – men's Canoe Single (C1) 200m**
Ivan Shtyl (Russia) 40.346
**Canoe Sprint – men's Kayak Single (K1) 200m**
Ed McKeever (Great Britain) 35.087

## Team GB moment of the day
Great Britain's women's Hockey team bounced back from their 2-1 semi-fin
defeat to Argentina to gain the consolation of bronze thanks to victory ove
New Zealand on Day 14 at the Riverbank Arena. For captain Kate Walsh,
it marked a remarkable turnaround as the 32-year-old led her team to a 3-
win courtesy of goals from Alex Danson, Crista Cullen and Sarah Thomas.
In Team GB's first group game against Japan, Walsh fractured her jaw whe
she was hit by a stick and had to have surgery to insert a titanium plate to
stabilise the area in her face. Just six days later she was back in group act
against China, before leading her side to the podium with the win over the
Kiwis at the end of the competition.

The medal equalled Britain's best ever performance in the women's Hock
event, matching the bronze they won 20 years earlier at the Barcelona 19
Olympic Games.

## Golden Games moment
Tunisia's Oussama Mellouli made history for the second Olympic Games
running when he won the men's 10km Marathon Swim in Hyde Park. At
Beijing 2008, Mellouli became the first African male to win an individual
Olympic Swimming title with his success in the 1500m Freestyle. Victory ir
The Serpentine saw him become the first swimmer to win an Olympic meda
both in the pool and in open water at the same Games following his bronz
medal earlier in the London 2012 programme in the 1500m Freestyle ever
at the Aquatics Centre.

Apart from the second lap, after which he emerged in sixth place, the
28-year-old was never out of the top three in what was an imperious
performance, although he admitted afterwards: 'I was really worried towa
the end. The last 400 metres I basically went through hell and came back
to life. My shoulders were getting so heavy and my legs were so tight and
my lungs were burning so much.' ■

# Day 15

## Saturday, 11 August 2012

## Going for gold

**Athletics**
Women's 800m • Men's 5000m • Men's 4 x 100m Relay • Women's 4 x 400m Relay • Women's High Jump • Men's Javelin Throw • Men's 50km Race Walk • Women's 20km Race Walk

**Basketball**
Women's Basketball

**Boxing**
Men's Light Fly Weight (46-49kg) • Men's Bantam Weight (-56kg) Men's Light Welter Weight (-64kg) • Men's Middle Weight (-75kg) • Men's Heavy Weight (-91kg)

**Canoe Sprint**
Men's Kayak Single (K1) 200m • Men's Canoe Single (C1) 200m • Women's Kayak Single (K1) 200m • Men's Kayak Double (K2) 200m

**Cycling – Mountain Bike**
Women's Cross-Country

**Diving**
Men's 10m Platform

**Football**
Men's Football

**Gymnastics – Rhythmic**
Individual All-Around Competition

**Handball**
Women's Handball

**Hockey**
Men's Hockey

**Modern Pentathlon**
Men's Individual Competition

**Sailing**
Women's Match Racing (Elliott 6m)

**Taekwondo**
Women's +67kg • Men's +80kg

**Volleyball**
Women's Volleyball

**Wrestling**
Men's Freestyle 120 kg • Men's Freestyle 60 kg • Men's Freestyle 84 kg

**Right:** The Olympic Stadium reached fever pitch as Mo Farah added the 5000m gold medal to the 10,000m title he won a week earlier

# A day of champions 11 August 2012

**The end of the Games was in sight but there were more gold medals to be won than on any other day at London 2012 as Mo Farah and Usain Bolt provided a suitably momentous finish to the action inside the Olympic Stadium.**

The golden moments kept on coming as the penultimate day of London 2012 delivered excitement by the minute and for Great Britain's Mo Farah it saw him take his place in Olympic history.

In what was the busiest single day of the Games in terms of medal action, with 32 golds being awarded, Farah claimed victory in the 5000m exactly one week after winning the 10,000m title at the Olympic Stadium. The 29-year-old produced a tactically-astute display to become the seventh man to complete the long-distance double at the Games. Roared on by what was described as a 'wall of noise' from

the 80,000-strong crowd, Farah hit the front with 700 metres remaining and, despite being challenged in the closing stages, he held on for the win before celebrating with his trademark 'Mobot' pose.

That performance was always going to be hard to top, but if there was one man at the Games capable of trying it was Usain Bolt. Having won all three sprint titles on offer in Beijing four years earlier, and with the 100m and 200m gold medals already in the bag from London 2012, the sprinting superstar completed another treble in emphatic style by running the anchor leg to help Jamaica beat the United States to win the 4 x 100m Relay

in a new world record of 36.84. Allyson Felix also won her third gold medal of the Games to help the USA to victory in the women's 4 x 400m Relay. Other Olympic champions on the last day of Athletics action were Russian Federation's Mariya Savinova and Anna Chicherova in the women's 800m and women's High Jump respectively, while Trinidad and Tobago's 19-year-old Keshorn Walcott was a surprise winner of the men's Javelin Throw with 84.58.

In the men's Boxing finals at ExCeL, the noise in the arena was deafening as Team GB's Luke Campbell and Ireland's John Joe Nevin fought for glory in the Bantam Weight (-56kg) division. The two fighters were evenly matched after two rounds with Campbell leading by a single point, but the Hull man then landed a superb left-hand counter in the final round to floor his opponent as he went on to secure Britain's first gold in the event since 1908 thanks to a 14-11 victory. Shiming Zou of China retained his Light Fly Weight (46-49kg) title, with the other golds on the night going to Cuba's Roniel Iglesias (Light Welter Weight), Japan's Ryota Murata (Middle Weight) and Ukraine's Oleksandr Usyk (Heavy Weight).

Great Britain's Tom Daley showed resilience to come through difficult times to earn a bronze medal in the men's 10m Platform Diving

**‘It's unbelievable. Two gold medals, who would have thought that? It's been a long journey of grafting and grafting ’**

*Team GB's Mo Farah on winning gold in the 5000m and 10,000m*

**Above:** Great Britain's Luke Campbell came through a close bout with Irish rival John Joe Nevin to win the Bantam Weight Boxing gold medal

**Below:** Mo Farah and Usain Bolt try out each other's trademark poses after winning on the final night of Athletics action at the Olympic Stadium

**Right:** Russian athlete Anna Chicherova shows her delight after her gold medal-winning success at 2.05 in the women's High Jump

**Below:** Teenager Keshorn Walcott upset the odds when he won the men's Javelin Throw for Trinidad and Tobago with a national record throw of 84.58

The Aquatics Centre witnessed a dramatic men's 10m Platform Diving final as London 2012 poster boy Tom Daley clinched a bronze medal for Team GB and David Boudia of the USA upset world champion and favourite Bo Qiu by beating the Chinese star into second place. For 18-year-old Daley, the medal marked a fine recovery after being allowed to re-take his first dive after complaining he had been distracted by camera flashes from the crowd. The Plymouth teenager produced superb scores for his fourth and fifth dives to lead by 0.15 points going into the last round. Daley then achieved a single score of 10 for his final back dive, but as it had a lower degree of difficulty than his rivals' it allowed Boudia to score higher and claim a surprise win.

In total 21 different countries claimed gold on the third Saturday of the Games and it was perhaps fitting that it was the host nation that got the ball rolling just after 9.30am. On the last day of the Canoe Sprint at Eton Dorney, Britain's Ed McKeever stormed to gold in the men's Kayak Single (K1) 200m as, despite battling a headwind, he made a fantastic start and powered over the line ahead of his rivals. Next up was the men's Canoe Single (C1) 200m, which was won by Ukrainian Yuri Cheban, before New Zealand's Lisa Carrington was victorious in the women's Kayak Single (K1) 200m final. There was further medal success for Great Britain in the men's Kayak Double (K2) 200m as Jon Schofield and Liam Heath claimed bronze behind the gold-winning Russian pair of Yury Postrigay and Alexander Dyachenko.

## Walk of fame

On a successful day for Russia, more glory followed in the final of the men's 50km Race Walk as Sergey Kirdyapkin set a new Olympic record, before Evgeniya Kanaeva became the first rhythmic gymnast to defend an Olympic title thanks to a series of breathtaking performances in the Individual All-Round Competition. A dominant display of a different kind was seen at the women's Mountain Bike Cycling event, where Julie Bresset of France led from the gun to beat Sabine Spitz of Germany by over a minute as the Beijing 2008 champion had to settle for silver.

Spanish skipper Tamara Echegoyen and her crew-mates Sofia Toro and Angela Pumariega were too good for favourites Australia in the women's Match Racing Sailing final, while there was another shock soon after in the men's Football gold medal match as Mexico scored inside 30 seconds on their way to a 2-1 win over Brazil.

As Day 15 moved into the evening session, a bumper night of sporting brilliance begun in superb fashion as Elena Lashmanova of Russia broke the world record in winning the women's 20km Race Walk on the streets of London. In the men's Freestyle Wrestling finals, Azerbaijan won two gold medals with Toghrul Asgarov triumphing in the 60kg and Sharif Sharifov in the 84kg. The night, however, belonged to Artur Taymazov of Uzbekistan as he became the first wrestler to win three successive gold medals at the Games in the 120kg division – doing so by not dropping a single point during the competition. In the men's Modern Pentathlon, David Svoboda of the Czech Republic overhauled China's Zhongrong Cao on the final 1km lap of the combined run and shoot to claim a thrilling victory at Greenwich Park. In the women's Volleyball, Brazil retained their Olympic title courtesy of a 3-1 win against the United States, while Germany defended their men's Hockey crown by seeing off the Netherlands 2-1 in a competition that saw Australia claim bronze after beating Great Britain 3-1. Norway won the women's Handball gold thanks to a 26-23 triumph over Montenegro and the United States saw off France 86-50 in the women's Basketball final. The last medals of a memorable day came in the Taekwondo as Serbia's Milica Mandic took the honours in the women's +67kg and Carlo Molfetta of Italy won the men's +80kg competition after beating Anthony Obame, whose silver was a first Olympic medal for Gabon.

Jan Philipp Rabente scores for Germany against the Netherlands in the men's Hockey final

Usain Bolt collected his third gold medal – for the second successive Games – when he anchored Jamaica's 4 x 100m Relay team to victory in a world record time

**Above left:** Candace Parker shoots during the United States' win over France in the women's Basketball final

**Left:** Artur Taymazov of Uzbekistan (in red) earned his third Wrestling gold

**Below:** The women's 20km Race Walk was won in world record time by Russia's Elena Lashmanova

**Above:** Julie Bresset of France heads for gold in the women's Mountain Bike at Hadleigh Farm in Essex

**Right:** Men's Modern Pentathlon gold and silver winners David Svoboda and Zhongrong Cao

**Below:** Ed McKeever celebrates winning the men's Kayak Single (K1) 200m

# For the record

## World records
**Athletics – women's 20km Race Walk**
Elena Lashmanova (Russia) 1:25.02
**Athletics – men's 4 x 100m Relay**
Jamaica 36.84

## Olympic records
**Athletics – men's 50km Race Walk**
Sergey Kirdyapkin (Russia) 3:35.59

❝ **It's an Olympic medal. An Olympic bronze medal is equal to a gold in any other competition** ❞

*Great Britain's Diving bronze-medallist Tom Daley*

## Team GB moment of the day
Mo Farah became the first Briton in history to win the Olympic 5000m title, with his sensational performance in the final coming just a week after he had become the first British athlete to win the 10,000m at the Games. Farah had brought the curtain down on 'Super Saturday' a week earlier for Team GB with his first victory. His second was equally as special for the host nation fans inside the Olympic Stadium.

The 29-year-old showed great maturity to position himself in exactly the right place during the final lap, which he covered in under 53 seconds. Farah looked a picture of disbelief as he crossed the line to put his name in the record books alongside legends of the sport Hannes Kolehmainen, Emil Zatopek, Vladimir Kuts, Lasse Viren, Miruts Yifter and Kenenisa Bekele in having completed the long-distance double on the track. Farah's victory also meant Great Britain had won four Athletics golds at an Olympic Games for the first time in 32 years.

## Golden Games moment
Mexico secured arguably the greatest triumph in their Football history as they upset pre-tournament favourites Brazil with a 2-1 win in the men's final to claim gold for the first time in the event. Oribe Peralta wrote his name into Mexican folklore with a deadly double against the Brazilians, who many believed were destined to finally end their wait for Olympic glory.

In front of a crowd of 86,162 at Wembley Stadium, Peralta gave his team a dream start by firing home after only 28 seconds to record the fastest ever goal in the final of a FIFA tournament. Brazil were much improved in the second half but fell further behind when in-form striker Peralta netted with a bullet header from Marco Fabian's free-kick. Hulk pulled a goal back in stoppage time and the game was almost taken into extra time, only for Oscar to miss a last-gasp effort from close range as Mexico held on for a famous victory. ■

❝ **It sounds stupid but it's not elation, more relief, and I'm so happy to do it front of a home crowd** ❞

*Great Britain's Ed McKeever after powering to victory in the Men's Kayak Single (K1) 200m*

# Day 16

Sunday, 12 August 2012

## Going for gold

**Athletics**
Men's Marathon

**Basketball**
Men's Basketball

**Boxing**
Men's Fly Weight (-52kg) • Men's Light Weight (-60kg) •
Men's Welter Weight (-69kg) • Men's Light Heavy Weight
(-81kg) • Men's Super Heavy Weight (+91kg)

**Cycling – Mountain Bike**
Men's Cross-Country

**Gymnastics – Rhythmic**
Group All-Around Competition

**Handball**
Men's Handball

**Modern Pentathlon**
Women's Individual Competition

**Volleyball**
Men's Volleyball

**Water Polo**
Men's Water Polo

**Wrestling**
Men's Freestyle 66kg • Men's Freestyle 96kg

**Right:** Anthony Joshua won Great Britain's
final gold medal of the Games when he
beat defending Olympic champion Roberto
Cammarelle in the men's Boxing Super
Heavy Weight (+91kg) final

# A fitting finale

**It was very much a case of last but not least on Day 16 as some enthralling climaxes in the likes of Boxing, Volleyball and Modern Pentathlon ensured a suitably dramatic conclusion to the Games.**

The London 2012 sporting extravaganza ended on a high as the last day of action provided some of the most thrilling moments of the Games.

With 287 Olympic champions already crowned, Day 16 had a lot to live up to following the magical memories that had come before it, but there was no let-up and the drama continued right up until the last event.

A third of the medals to be awarded on the final day were at ExCeL as 10,000 Boxing fans were treated to some incredible fights as the men's tournament came to a close. The highlight for the home fans came in the final of the Super Heavy Weight category, where London's very own Anthony Joshua stormed back from a three-point deficit in the last round to see off reigning Olympic champion Roberto Cammarelle via countback after a dramatic 18-18 draw. The 22-year-old produced a super-human effort to come from behind and admitted afterwards he had been inspired by his favourite film *300*, about Spartan warriors, as he blazed out for the final round against the legendary Italian. A latecomer to the sport just four years earlier, Joshua's brilliant gold medal also put the seal on the finest performance by a Great Britain Boxing team at the Games for over a century and saw them finish top of the medals table in the sport ahead of traditional super-powers such as Cuba, Ukraine and the Russian Federation.

Team-mate Fred Evans contributed to the tally of five medals for Team GB, although it was not the colour he had been hoping for as he had to settle for silver in the Welter Weight (-69kg) division. Evans had disposed of world champion and world number one Taras Shelestyuk in the semi-finals but was no match for Kazakhstan's Serik Sapiyev, who produced an incredible display to win 17-9 before picking up the prestigious Val Barker Trophy for best boxer of the Games. Cuban teenager Robeisy Ramirez Carrazana got the ball rolling in the first final of the afternoon by winning the Fly Weight (-52kg) title, before Ukraine's Vasyl Lomachenko won the second Olympic gold medal of his career by outclassing Soonchul Han

Uganda's Stephen Kiprotich was an unexpected winner of the men's Marathon

> **My legs were screaming but I kept throwing punches in there and kept pushing to the final bell**
>
> *Team GB Super Heavy Weight Boxing gold medallist Anthony Joshua*

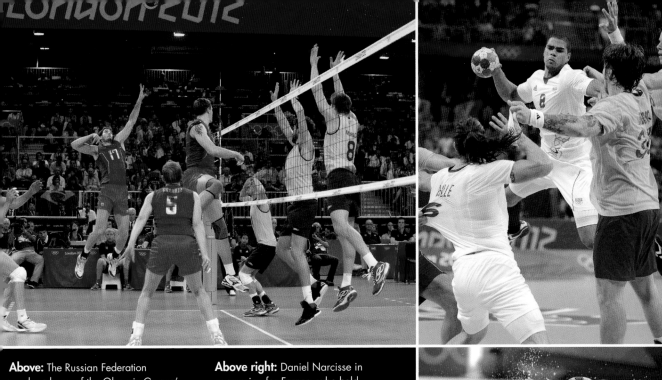

**Above:** The Russian Federation produced one of the Olympic Games' great fightbacks to beat Brazil in the final of the men's Volleyball

**Above right:** Daniel Narcisse in possession for France, who held off a fierce challenge from Sweden in the men's Handball final

**Below:** The gruelling men's Mountain Bike Cross-Country race was won in a sprint to the line by Jaroslav Kulhavy

**Right:** Miho Boskovic in action during Croatia's win over Italy in the final of the men's Water Polo

of Korea 19-9 in the Light Weight (-60kg) category. A compelling day of action in the ring saw a second draw decided on countback, with Russian Egor Mekhontcev handed the verdict against Kazakhstan's Adilbek Niyazymbetov in the men's Light Heavy Weight (-81kg) final after the fight ended 15-15.

There was also excitement aplenty at Hadleigh Farm as the men's Mountain Bike Cross-Country race came down to a sprint finish between Jaroslav Kulhavy of the Czech Republic and Switzerland's Nino Schurter after almost an hour and a half of racing around the technically difficult course. With the 2004 and 2008 champion Julien Absalon of France out of the running following a puncture early in the race, it was left to Kulhavy to grab the initiative on the penultimate bend to get the better of Schurter by the narrowest of margins and win the gold.

The men's Volleyball final at Earls Court was equally thrilling as the Russian Federation came from two sets down to beat Brazil 3-2, while France became the first country to retain the Olympic title in men's Handball following a tense 22-21 victory in the final against Sweden – holding on in the closing stages as the Scandinavians threatened to complete a late comeback.

Croatia secured their first men's Water Polo Olympic gold medal thanks to an 8-6 win over Italy to cement their place as the outstanding Water Polo side of the London 2012 tournament, with eight wins from the eight matches they played as 38-year-old skipper Samir Barac inspired his side to glory in his last match before retiring from international competition.

## USA run close

There were no surprises in the men's Basketball final as the United States bagged the Olympic title for the 14th time, although they did not have it all their own way as they had when beating Argentina 109-83 in their semi-final two days earlier. In Spain they met an opponent eager to go one better than four years earlier when they had to settle for silver and it proved to be the second closest final in Olympic history before the USA triumphed 107-100, with Kevin Durant scoring 30 points for the champions. Kobe Bryant contributed 17 points as he signed off from international Basketball with the second Olympic gold medal of his career. 'This is right at the top of my achievements,' said the Los Angeles Lakers star. 'We got the gold twice. What else can I ask for?'

Another big favourite to land gold were the Russian Federation in the Rhythmic Gymnastics Group All-Around Competition and they did not disappoint, with their two stunning routines earning them a fourth consecutive Olympic title in the event and helping to see off the challenge of Belarus in second and Italy in third.

It was not a day for the favourites, however, in the men's Marathon which saw thousands of people turn out on the streets of London to cheer home the surprise winner from Uganda. Stephen Kiprotich stunned the Kenyan challenge to clinch only his country's second ever Olympic gold, coming 40 years after John Akii-Bua's triumph in the 400m Hurdles. The 23-year-old burst past the two Kenyan favourites, reigning world champion Abel Kirui and Wilson Kipsang Kiprotich (no relation), around the 38km mark and left them trailing in his wake to win in 2:08.01. Kirui finished 26 seconds later to take silver, with Wilson Kipsang Kiprotich winning bronze. The three athletes had the added honour of receiving their medals at the Closing Ceremony as is customary at the Games.

Also at ExCeL, Japan won their first men's Wrestling gold in 24 years after Tatsuhiro Yonemitsu defeated India's Sushil Kumar in the final of the 66kg Freestyle division, while Jake Varner became the second USA wrestler to top the podium at the Games after beating Ukraine's Valerii Andriitsev 1-0 1-0 in the 96kg final.

The final gold medallist of London 2012 was Lithuanian Laura Asadauskaite, who produced a fine performance to win the women's Modern Pentathlon at Greenwich Park, with Great Britain's Samantha Murray earning the silver medal ahead of Yane Marques of Brazil.

Tatsuhiro Yonemitsu of Japan beat India's Sushil Kumar in the Freestyle Wrestling 66kg final

The Russian Federation made a colourful splash on the final day with their fourth successive Olympic title in the Rhythmic Gymnastics Group Competition

**Above:** Kazakhstan's Serik Sapiyev overcame Freddie Evans in the Men's Welter Weight (-69kg) final

**Right:** The men's Marathon goes through Leadenhall Market on a course designed to show off some of central London's most iconic sights

**Below:** Lithuanian Laura Asadauskaite won the last gold medal of the Games in the women's Modern Pentathlon

**Below right:** Kevin Durant top-scored with 30 points in the United States' win over Spain in the men's Basketball

London 2012

# For the record

❝ **The stadium erupted when I came in every time and my legs just picked up. I kind of wish now there was more to run because I was enjoying myself so much** ❞

*Great Britain's Samantha Murray after winning a silver medal in the Modern Pentathlon*

## Team GB moment of the day

Samantha Murray was the winner of Great Britain's last medal of London 2012 to help the host nation complete their most successful Olympic Games for 108 years on a tally of 65 medals, including 29 golds. It was a remarkable triumph for the 22-year-old from Clitheroe in Lancashire, who had considered walking away from the sport of Modern Pentathlon completely in 2008 and took a two-year break.

Murray recovered brilliantly from losing her first seven fencing bouts in the first event of the competition and sat fourth overall going into the final discipline, the combined run and shoot, following good showings in the swimming and equestrian jumping. She then managed to overhaul Brazil's Yane Marques and Amelie Caze of France to claim a surprise silver behind Lithuanian winner Laura Asadauskaite. Murray, who was ranked only 78th in the world in February, continued Britain's great success in the women's Modern Pentathlon and ensured they have won medals at every Games since its first introduction at Sydney 2000.

## Golden Games moment

The Russian Federation produced one of the all-time great Olympic Volleyball comebacks to take gold against Brazil at Earls Court. The title seemed destined to head to South America after the Brazilians won the first two sets, led 22-19 in third set and had two match points. However, the Russians produced a momentous fightback that saw them become the first side to win gold from two sets down in the men's competition in Olympic history.

Inspired by the 2.18m-tall Dmitriy Muserskiy, who bagged a match-winning 31-point haul in a superb performance at the net, the Russians went on to seal a 19-25, 20-25, 29-27, 25-22, 15-9 victory which means they have won medals in the sport at four successive Games. Sergey Tetyukhin was competing in his fifth Olympic Games at the age of 36 and added a gold to his collection of one silver and two bronzes to end his international career on a high. ∎

❝ **It was really hard, because we went full-gas the whole time. I gave everything for this race** ❞

*Jaroslav Kulhavy of the Czech Republic on beating Switzerland's Nino Schurter in a thrilling sprint finish in the men's Mountain Bike Cross-Country race*

# Time to party

**With the sporting action all over, it was time to celebrate the end of London 2012 and some of the UK's biggest musical acts provided the soundtrack as the honour of hosting the Games was passed to Rio de Janeiro**

After all the hard-fought sporting action was over, it was party time at the Olympic Stadium as London 2012 came to a breathtaking finale at the Closing Ceremony.

The best of Great Britain's past and present music scene performed for the world as the host city put on the concert of a lifetime to glorify the memorable moments created during London's third staging of the Olympic Games. Aimed at celebrating one of Britain's strongest cultural exports over the last 50 years, the stunning musical extravaganza featured stars such as Annie Lennox, the Spice Girls, Madness, the Kaiser Chiefs and Queen, and culminated with a glimpse of the carnival that awaits in Rio de Janeiro in four years' time.

Entering the Stadium, the audience was treated to a vision of working London wrapped in newspaper as they were taken to the heart of the capital's busy rush hour, before singer Emeli Sandé delighted the crowds with hit song *Read All About It* to kick things off. Winston Churchill, played by actor Timothy Spall, then stood atop Big Ben reciting the same lines from Shakespeare's *The Tempest* which helped open the Games at the Opening Ceremony: 'Be not afeard: the isle is full of noises.'

Among the highlights to follow was the sight of percussion group Stomp swinging from scaffolding, playing models of the capital's landmarks including Big Ben and the London Eye as if they were instruments. The Kinks' frontman Ray Davies arrived in a black cab to sing his 1960s hit *Waterloo Sunset*, while many of the competing athletes flooded into the field of play by coming through the crowd to form a mosh pit around the stage. The 70,000 Games Makers were honoured with a shower of petals and Monty Python comedian Eric Idle led the crowd in a version of *Always Look On The Bright Side of Life* while being joined by dancing performers that included skating nuns.

After the Olympic Flag was lowered and presented to Rio de Janeiro Mayor Eduardo Paes, it was time for a samba party delivered as a taster of what is to come in 2016. After speeches by LOCOG Chair Seb Coe and President of the International Olympic Committee Jacques Rogge, Take That performed *Rule the World* before celebrated ballerina Darcey Bussell flew into the Stadium as part of the ritual of extinguishing the Olympic Flame. At this point the Games were over, but not before the Closing Ceremony provided one last chance to get in the party spirit as The Who brought the curtain down on London 2012, which Rogge described as 'unforgettable' in his words of praise during his speech to bring the Olympic Games to a close.

He said: 'These were happy and glorious Games. We will never forget the smiles, the kindness and the support of the wonderful volunteers, the much-needed heroes of these Games. You, the spectators and the public, provided the soundtrack for these Games. Your enthusiastic cheers energised the competitors and brought a festive spirit to every Olympic venue. You have shown the world the best of British hospitality.'

The Closing Ceremony saw the Olympic Flag passed to the Mayor of Rio de Janeiro

**Above:** Featuring models of London's most famous landmarks, the Closing Ceremony was a stunning spectacle of sight and sound

**Left:** A phoenix soars above the Stadium as the Olympic Flame is extinguished, marking the formal end of the Games

**Below:** Athletes from around the world gather at the centre of the Olympic Stadium to create a multi-coloured scene during the Closing Ceremony

Athletes and spectators alike were dazzled by the spectacular fireworks display at the climax of the Closing Ceremony

# Games statistics

## The Games by numbers

London 2012 witnessed some incredible sporting achievements and the record books were rewritten on many occasions as athletes brought the Olympic motto to life by going faster, higher and stronger than ever before.

The medal table charts the success of each nation, with 85 countries having their flag raised at least once at one of the many stunning venues at London 2012.

The USA finished top of the standings with 46 golds and an overall tally of 104, with China second on 88, 38 of which were gold.

It was also a glorious Games for third-placed Great Britain as the Host Nation's athletes responded in style to the patriotic support they received from the fans, who flocked in huge numbers to get a glimpse of their heroes at every opportunity.

Team GB finished with 29 golds and 65 in total – their best haul in 104 years – as the likes of Mo Farah, Jessica Ennis and Chris Hoy all delivered when the pressure was on.

Regardless of the nationality, behind every medallist was a story of hard work, determination and a journey which ended on the London 2012 podium.

**Right:** Usain Bolt's new Olympic record of 9.63 in retaining his men's 100m title was among the many amazing achievements seen by fans at London 2012

# Medal count by country

**Above:** All-time Olympic Swimming great Michael Phelps won four of the USA's 46 gold medals

**Below:** Rohullah Nikpah won Taekwondo bronze for Afghanistan

| | Country | Gold | Silver | Bronze | Total |
|---|---|---|---|---|---|
| 1 | United States | 46 | 29 | 29 | 104 |
| 2 | China | 38 | 27 | 23 | 88 |
| 3 | Great Britain | 29 | 17 | 19 | 65 |
| 4 | Russian Federation | 24 | 26 | 32 | 82 |
| 5 | Republic of Korea | 13 | 8 | 7 | 28 |
| 6 | Germany | 11 | 19 | 14 | 44 |
| 7 | France | 11 | 11 | 12 | 34 |
| 8 | Italy | 8 | 9 | 11 | 28 |
| 9 | Hungary | 8 | 4 | 5 | 17 |
| 10 | Australia | 7 | 16 | 12 | 35 |
| 11 | Japan | 7 | 14 | 17 | 38 |
| 12 | Kazakhstan | 7 | 1 | 5 | 13 |
| 13 | Netherlands | 6 | 6 | 8 | 20 |
| 14 | Ukraine | 6 | 5 | 9 | 20 |
| 15 | New Zealand | 6 | 2 | 5 | 13 |
| 16 | Cuba | 5 | 3 | 6 | 14 |
| 17 | Iran | 4 | 5 | 3 | 12 |
| 18 | Jamaica | 4 | 4 | 4 | 12 |
| 19 | Czech Republic | 4 | 3 | 3 | 10 |
| 20 | DPR Korea | 4 | 0 | 2 | 6 |
| 21 | Spain | 3 | 10 | 4 | 17 |
| 22 | Brazil | 3 | 5 | 9 | 17 |
| 23 | Belarus | 1 | 5 | 5 | 11 |
| 24 | South Africa | 3 | 2 | 1 | 6 |
| 25 | Ethiopia | 3 | 1 | 3 | 7 |
| 26 | Croatia | 3 | 1 | 2 | 6 |
| 27 | Romania | 2 | 5 | 2 | 9 |
| 28 | Kenya | 2 | 4 | 5 | 11 |
| 29 | Denmark | 2 | 4 | 3 | 9 |
| 30 | Azerbaijan | 2 | 2 | 6 | 10 |
| 30 | Poland | 2 | 2 | 6 | 10 |
| 32 | Turkey | 2 | 2 | 1 | 5 |
| 33 | Switzerland | 2 | 2 | 0 | 4 |
| 34 | Lithuania | 2 | 1 | 2 | 5 |
| 35 | Norway | 2 | 1 | 1 | 4 |
| 36 | Canada | 1 | 5 | 12 | 18 |
| 37 | Sweden | 1 | 4 | 3 | 8 |
| 38 | Colombia | 1 | 3 | 4 | 8 |
| 39 | Georgia | 1 | 3 | 3 | 7 |
| 39 | Mexico | 1 | 3 | 3 | 7 |
| 41 | Ireland | 1 | 1 | 3 | 5 |
| 42 | Argentina | 1 | 1 | 2 | 4 |
| 42 | Slovenia | 1 | 1 | 2 | 4 |

| Country | Gold | Silver | Bronze | Total |
|---|---|---|---|---|
| 42 Serbia | 1 | 1 | 2 | 4 |
| 45 Tunisia | 1 | 1 | 1 | 3 |
| 46 Dominican Rep. | 1 | 1 | 0 | 2 |
| 47 Trinidad & Tobago | 1 | 0 | 3 | 4 |
| 47 Uzbekistan | 1 | 0 | 3 | 4 |
| 49 Latvia | 1 | 0 | 1 | 2 |
| 50 Algeria | 1 | 0 | 0 | 1 |
| 50 Bahamas | 1 | 0 | 0 | 1 |
| 50 Grenada | 1 | 0 | 0 | 1 |
| 50 Uganda | 1 | 0 | 0 | 1 |
| 50 Venezuela | 1 | 0 | 0 | 1 |
| 55 India | 0 | 2 | 4 | 6 |
| 56 Mongolia | 0 | 2 | 3 | 5 |
| 57 Thailand | 0 | 2 | 1 | 3 |
| 58 Egypt | 0 | 2 | 0 | 2 |
| 59 Slovakia | 0 | 1 | 3 | 4 |
| 60 Armenia | 0 | 1 | 2 | 3 |
| 60 Belgium | 0 | 1 | 2 | 3 |
| 60 Finland | 0 | 1 | 2 | 3 |
| 63 Bulgaria | 0 | 1 | 1 | 2 |
| 63 Estonia | 0 | 1 | 1 | 2 |
| 63 Indonesia | 0 | 1 | 1 | 2 |
| 63 Malaysia | 0 | 1 | 1 | 2 |
| 63 Puerto Rico | 0 | 1 | 1 | 2 |
| 63 Chinese Taipei | 0 | 1 | 1 | 2 |
| 69 Botswana | 0 | 1 | 0 | 1 |
| 69 Cyprus | 0 | 1 | 0 | 1 |
| 69 Gabon | 0 | 1 | 0 | 1 |
| 69 Guatemala | 0 | 1 | 0 | 1 |
| 69 Montenegro | 0 | 1 | 0 | 1 |
| 69 Portugal | 0 | 1 | 0 | 1 |
| 75 Greece | 0 | 0 | 2 | 2 |
| 75 Rep. of Moldova | 0 | 0 | 2 | 2 |
| 75 Qatar | 0 | 0 | 2 | 2 |
| 75 Singapore | 0 | 0 | 2 | 2 |
| 79 Afghanistan | 0 | 0 | 1 | 1 |
| 79 Bahrain | 0 | 0 | 1 | 1 |
| 79 Hong Kong | 0 | 0 | 1 | 1 |
| 79 Saudi Arabia | 0 | 0 | 1 | 1 |
| 79 Kuwait | 0 | 0 | 1 | 1 |
| 79 Morocco | 0 | 0 | 1 | 1 |
| 79 Tajikistan | 0 | 0 | 1 | 1 |

**Above:** Erick Barrondo's silver in the 20km Race Walk was Guatamala's first ever Olympic medal

**Below:** Light Fly Weight boxer Shiming Zou helped China into second place

# Event results

## Archery

### Men's Individual
| | | |
|---|---|---|
| Gold | Jin Hyek Oh (Republic of Korea) | |
| Silver | Takaharu Furukawa (Japan) | |
| Bronze | Xiaoxiang Dai (China) | |

### Women's Individual
| | | |
|---|---|---|
| Gold | Bo Bae Ki (Republic of Korea) | |
| Silver | Aida Roman (Mexico) | |
| Bronze | Mariana Avitia (Mexico) | |

### Men's Team
| | |
|---|---|
| Gold | Italy (Michele Frangilli, Marco Galiazzo, Mauro Nespoli) |
| Silver | United States (Brady Ellison, Jacob Wuki, Jake Kaminski) |
| Bronze | Republic of Korea (Im Dong-hyun, Kim Bubmin Oh Jin-hyek) |

### Women's Team
| | |
|---|---|
| Gold | Korea (Hyeonju Choi, Bo Bae Ki, Sung Jin Lee) |
| Silver | China (Ming Cheng, Yuting Fang, Jing Xu) |
| Bronze | Japan (Ren Hayakawa, Miki Kanie, Kaori Kawanaka) |

## Athletics

### Men's 100m
| | | |
|---|---|---|
| Gold | Usain Bolt (Jamaica) | 9.63 [OR] |
| Silver | Yohan Blake (Jamaica) | 9.75 |
| Bronze | Justin Gatlin (USA) | 9.79 |

### Men's 200m
| | | |
|---|---|---|
| Gold | Usain Bolt (Jamaica) | 19.32 |
| Silver | Yohan Blake (Jamaica) | 19.44 |
| Bronze | Warren Weir (Jamaica) | 19.84 |

### Men's 400m
| | | |
|---|---|---|
| Gold | Kirani James (Grenada) | 43.94 |
| Silver | Luguelin Santos (Dominican Rep) | 44.46 |
| Bronze | Lalonde Gordon (Trinidad & T) | 44.52 |

### Men's 800m
| | | |
|---|---|---|
| Gold | David Rudisha (Kenya) | 1:40.91 [WR] |
| Silver | Nijel Amos (Botswana) | 1:41.73 |
| Bronze | Timothy Kitum (Kenya) | 1:42.53 |

### Men's 1500m
| | | |
|---|---|---|
| Gold | Taoufik Makhloufi (Algeria) | 3:34.08 |
| Silver | Leonel Manzano (USA) | 3:34.79 |
| Bronze | Abdalaati Iguider (Morocco) | 3:35.13 |

### Men's 5000m
| | | |
|---|---|---|
| Gold | Mo Farah (GBR) | 13:41.66 |
| Silver | Dejen Gebremeskel (Ethiopia) | 13:41.98 |
| Bronze | Thomas Longosiwa (Kenya) | 13:42.36 |

### Men's 10,000m
| | | |
|---|---|---|
| Gold | Mo Farah (GBR) | 27:30.42 |
| Silver | Galen Rupp (USA) | 27:30.90 |
| Bronze | Tariku Bekele (Ethiopia) | 27:31.43 |

### Men's Marathon
| | | |
|---|---|---|
| Gold | Stephen Kiprotich (Uganda) | 2:08:01 |
| Silver | Abel Kirui (Kenya) | 2:08:27 |
| Bronze | Wilson Kipsang Kiprotich (KEN) | 2:09:37 |

### Men's 3000m Steeplechase
| | | |
|---|---|---|
| Gold | Ezekiel Kemboi (Kenya) | 8:18.56 |
| Silver | Mahiedine Mekhissi-Benabbad (France) | 8:19.08 |
| Bronze | Abel Kiprop Mutai (Kenya) | 8:19.73 |

### Men's 110m Hurdles
| | | |
|---|---|---|
| Gold | Aries Merritt (USA) | 12.92 |
| Silver | Jason Richardson (USA) | 13.04 |
| Bronze | Hansle Parchment (Jamaica) | 13.12 |

### Men's 400m Hurdles
| | | |
|---|---|---|
| Gold | Felix Sanchez (Dominican Rep) | 47.63 |
| Silver | Michael Tinsley (USA) | 47.91 |
| Bronze | Javier Culson (Puerto Rico) | 48.10 |

### Men's High Jump
| | | |
|---|---|---|
| Gold | Ivan Ukhov (Russian Fed.) | 2.38 |
| Silver | Erik Kynard (USA) | 2.33 |
| Bronze | Mutaz Barshim (Qatar) | 2.29 |
| Bronze | Derek Drouin (Canada) | 2.29 |
| Bronze | Robert Grabarz (GBR) | 2.29 |

### Men's Pole Vault
| | | |
|---|---|---|
| Gold | Renaud Lavillenie (France) | 5.97 [OR] |
| Silver | Bjorn Otto (Germany) | 5.91 |
| Bronze | Raphael Holzdeppe (Germany) | 5.91 |

### Men's Long Jump
| | | |
|---|---|---|
| Gold | Greg Rutherford (GBR) | 8.31 |
| Silver | Mitchell Watt (Australia) | 8.16 |
| Bronze | Will Claye (USA) | 8.12 |

### Men's Triple Jump
| | | |
|---|---|---|
| Gold | Christian Taylor (USA) | 17.81 |
| Silver | Will Claye (USA) | 17.62 |
| Bronze | Fabrizio Donato (Italy) | 17.48 |

### Men's Shot Put
| | | |
|---|---|---|
| Gold | Tomasz Majewski (Poland) | 21.89 |
| Silver | David Storl (Germany) | 21.86 |
| Bronze | Reese Hoffa (USA) | 21.23 |

### Men's Discus Throw
| | | |
|---|---|---|
| Gold | Robert Harting (Germany) | 68.27 |
| Silver | Ehsan Hadadi (Iran) | 68.18 |
| Bronze | Gerd Kanter (Estonia) | 68.03 |

### Men's Hammer Throw
| | | |
|---|---|---|
| Gold | Krisztian Pars (Hungary) | 80.59 |
| Silver | Primoz Kozmus (Slovenia) | 79.36 |
| Bronze | Koji Murofushi (Japan) | 78.71 |

### Men's Javelin Throw
| | | |
|---|---|---|
| Gold | Keshorn Walcott (Trinidad & Tobago) | 84.58 |
| Silver | Oleksandr Pyatnytsya (Ukraine) | 84.51 |
| Bronze | Antti Ruuskanen (Finland) | 84.12 |

### Men's Decathlon
| | | |
|---|---|---|
| Gold | Ashton Eaton (USA) | 8869 |
| Silver | Trey Hardee (USA) | 8671 |
| Bronze | Leonel Suarez (Cuba) | 8523 |

### Men's 20km Race Walk
| | | |
|---|---|---|
| Gold | Ding Chen (China) | 1:18:46 [OR] |
| Silver | Erick Barrondo (Guatemala) | 1:18:57 |
| Bronze | Zhen Wang (China) | 1:19:25 |

### Men's 50km Race Walk
| | | |
|---|---|---|
| Gold | Sergey Kirdyapkin (Russian Fed.) | 3:35:59 [OR] |
| Silver | Jared Tallent (Australia) | 3:36:53 |
| Bronze | Tianfeng Si (China) | 3:37:16 |

### Men's 4 x 100m Relay
| | | |
|---|---|---|
| Gold | Jamaica | 36.84 [WR] |
| | (Nesta Carter, Michael Frater, Yohan Blake, Usain Bolt) | |
| Silver | United States | 37.04 |
| Bronze | Trinidad & Tobago | 38.12 |

### Men's 4 x 400m Relay
| | | |
|---|---|---|
| Gold | Bahamas | 2:56.72 |
| | (Chris Brown, Demetrius Pinder, Michael Mathie, Ramon Miller) | |
| Silver | United States | 2:57.05 |
| Bronze | Trinidad & Tobago | 2:59.40 |

### Women's 100m
| | | |
|---|---|---|
| Gold | Shelly-Ann Fraser-Pryce (Jamaica) | 10.75 |
| Silver | Carmelita Jeter (USA) | 10.78 |
| Bronze | Veronica Campbell-Brown (Jamaica) | 10.81 |

### Women's 200m
| | | |
|---|---|---|
| Gold | Allyson Felix (USA) | 21.88 |
| Silver | Shelly-Ann Fraser-Pryce (Jamaica) | 22.09 |
| Bronze | Carmelita Jeter (USA) | 22.14 |

### Women's 400m
| | | |
|---|---|---|
| Gold | Sanya Richards-Ross (USA) | 49.55 |
| Silver | Christine Ohuruogu (GBR) | 49.70 |
| Bronze | Deedee Trotter (USA) | 49.72 |

### Women's 800m
| | | |
|---|---|---|
| Gold | Mariya Savinova (Russian Fed.) | 1:56.19 |
| Silver | Caster Semenya (S Africa) | 1:57.23 |
| Bronze | Ekaterina Poistogova (Russian Fed.) | 1:57.53 |

### Women's 1500m
| | | |
|---|---|---|
| Gold | Asli Cakir Alptekin (Turkey) | 4:10.23 |
| Silver | Gamze Bulut (Turkey) | 4:10.40 |
| Bronze | Maryam Yusuf Jamal (Bahrain) | 4:10.74 |

### Women's 5000m
| | | |
|---|---|---|
| Gold | Meseret Defar (Ethiopia) | 15:4.25 |
| Silver | Vivian Cheruiyot (Kenya) | 15:04.73 |
| Bronze | Tirunesh Dibaba (Ethiopia) | 15:05.15 |

### Women's 10,000m
| | | |
|---|---|---|
| Gold | Tirunesh Dibaba (Ethiopia) | 30:20.75 |
| Silver | Sally Kipyego (Kenya) | 30:26.37 |
| Bronze | Vivian Cheruiyot (Kenya) | 30:30.44 |

### Women's Marathon
| | | |
|---|---|---|
| Gold | Tiki Gelana (Ethiopia) | 2:23:7 [OR] |
| Silver | Priscah Jeptoo (Kenya) | 2:23:12 |
| Bronze | Tatyana Arkhipova (Russian Fed.) | 2:23:29 |

### Women's 3000m Steeplechase
| | | |
|---|---|---|
| Gold | Yuliya Zaripova (Russian Fed.) | 9:6.72 |
| Silver | Habiba Ghribi (Tunisia) | 9:08.37 |
| Bronze | Sofia Assefa (Ethiopia) | 9:09.84 |

### Women's 100m Hurdles
| | | |
|---|---|---|
| Gold | Sally Pearson (Australia) | 12.35 [OR] |
| Silver | Dawn Harper (USA) | 12.37 |
| Bronze | Kellie Wells (USA) | 12.48 |

### Women's 400m Hurdles
| | | |
|---|---|---|
| Gold | Natalya Antyukh (Russian Fed.) | 52.70 |
| Silver | Lashinda Demus (USA) | 52.77 |
| Bronze | Zuzana Hejnova (Czech Rep) | 53.38 |

### Women's High Jump
| | | |
|---|---|---|
| Gold | Anna Chicherova (Russian Fed.) | 2.05 |
| Silver | Brigetta Barrett (USA) | 2.03 |
| Bronze | Svetlana Shkolina (Russian Fed.) | 2.03 |

Triple Jump winner
Christian Taylor

## Women's Pole Vault
| | | |
|---|---|---|
| Gold | Jennifer Suhr (USA) | 4.75 |
| Silver | Yarisley Silva (Cuba) | 4.75 |
| Bronze | Elena Isinbaeva (Russian Fed.) | 4.70 |

## Women's Long Jump
| | | |
|---|---|---|
| Gold | Brittney Reese (USA) | 7.12 |
| Silver | Elena Sokolova (Russian Fed.) | 7.07 |
| Bronze | Janay Deloach (USA) | 6.89 |

## Women's Triple Jump
| | | |
|---|---|---|
| Gold | Olga Rypakova (Kazakhstan) | 14.98 |
| Silver | Caterine Ibarguen (Colombia) | 14.80 |
| Bronze | Olha Saladuha (Ukraine) | 14.79 |

## Women's Shot Put
| | | |
|---|---|---|
| Gold | Valerie Adams (New Zealand) | 20.70 |
| Silver | Evgeniia Kolodko (Russian Fed.) | 20.48 |
| Bronze | Lijiao Gong (China) | 20.20 |

## Women's Discus Throw
| | | |
|---|---|---|
| Gold | Sandra Perkovic (Croatia) | 69.11 |
| Silver | Darya Pishchalnikova (Russian Fed.) | 67.56 |
| Bronze | Yanfeng Li (China) | 67.22 |

## Women's Hammer Throw
| | | |
|---|---|---|
| Gold | Tatyana Lysenko (Russian Fed.) | 78.18 [OR] |
| Silver | Anita Wlodarczyk (Poland) | 77.60 |
| Bronze | Betty Heidler (Germany) | 77.13 |

## Women's Javelin Throw
| | | |
|---|---|---|
| Gold | Barbora Spotakova (Czech Rep.) | 69.55 |
| Silver | Christina Obergfoll (Germany) | 65.16 |
| Bronze | Linda Stahl (Germany) | 64.91 |

## Women's Heptathlon
| | | |
|---|---|---|
| Gold | Jessica Ennis (GBR) | 6955 |
| Silver | Lilli Scwarzkopf (Germany) | 6649 |
| Bronze | Tatyana Chernova (Russian Fed.) | 6628 |

## Women's 20km Race Walk
| | | |
|---|---|---|
| Gold | Elena Lashmanova (Russian Fed.) | 1:25:2 [WR] |
| Silver | Olga Kaniskina (Russian Fed.) | 1:25:09 |
| Bronze | Shenjie Qieyang (China) | 1:25:16 |

## Women's 4 x 100m Relay
| | | |
|---|---|---|
| Gold | United States | 40.82 [WR] |
| | (Tianna Madison, Allyson Felix, Bianca Knight, Carmelita Jeter) | |
| Silver | Jamaica | 41.41 |
| Bronze | Ukraine | 42.04 |

## Women's 4 x 400m Relay
| | | |
|---|---|---|
| Gold | United States | 3:16.87 |
| | (DeeDee Trotter, Allyson Felix, Francena McCrory, Sanya Richards-Ross) | |
| Silver | Russian Fed | 3:20.23 |
| Bronze | Jamaica | 3:20.95 |

## Badminton

### Men's Singles
| | |
|---|---|
| Gold | Dan Lin (China) |
| Silver | Chong Wei Lee (Malaysia) |
| Bronze | Long Chen (China) |

### Women's Singles
| | |
|---|---|
| Gold | Xuerui Li (China) |
| Silver | Yihan Wang (China) |
| Bronze | Saina Nehwal (India) |

### Men's Doubles
| | |
|---|---|
| Gold | China (Yun Cai, Haifeng Fu) |
| Silver | Denmark (Mathias Boe, Carsten Mogensen) |
| Bronze | Rep of Korea (Jae Sung Chung, Yong Dae Lee) |

### Women's Doubles
| | |
|---|---|
| Gold | China (Qing Tian, Yunlei Zhao) |
| Silver | Japan (Fujii Mizuki, Kakiiwa Reika) |
| Bronze | Russian Fed (Valeria Sorokina, Nina Vislova) |

### Mixed Doubles
| | |
|---|---|
| Gold | China (Nan Zhang, Yunlei Zhao) |
| Silver | China (Chen Xu, Jin Ma) |
| Bronze | Denmark (Joachim Fischer, Christina Pedersen) |

## Basketball

**Men**
| | |
|---|---|
| Gold | United States |
| Silver | Spain |
| Bronze | Russian Federation |

**Women**
| | |
|---|---|
| Gold | United States |
| Silver | France |
| Bronze | Australia |

## Beach Volleyball

**Men**
| | |
|---|---|
| Gold | Germany (Julius Brink, Jonas Reckermann) |
| Silver | Brazil (Emanuelk rego, Alison Cerutti) |
| Bronze | Latvia (Martin Plavins, Janis Smedins) |

**Women**
| | |
|---|---|
| Gold | United States (Misty May-Treanor, Kerri Walsh) |
| Silver | United States (Jennifer Kessy, April Ross) |
| Bronze | Brazil (Larissa Franca, Juliana Silva) |

## Boxing

### Men's Light Fly Weight (49kg)
| | |
|---|---|
| Gold | Shiming Zou (China) |
| Silver | Kaeo Pongprayoon (Thailand) |
| Bronze | Paddy Barnes (Ireland) |
| Bronze | David Ayrapetyan (Russian Fed.) |

### Men's Fly Weight (52kg)
| | |
|---|---|
| Gold | Robeisy Ramirez Carrazana (Cuba) |
| Silver | Tugstsogt Nyambayar (Mongolia) |
| Bronze | Michael Conlon (Ireland) |
| Bronze | Misha Aloian (Russian Fed.) |

### Men's Bantam Weight (56kg)
| | |
|---|---|
| Gold | Luke Campbell (GBR) |
| Silver | John Joe Nevin (Ireland) |
| Bronze | Alvarez Estrada (Cuba) |
| Bronze | Satoshi Shimizu (Japan) |

### Men's Light Weight (60kg)
| | |
|---|---|
| Gold | Vasyl Lomachenko (Ukraine) |
| Silver | Soonchul Han (Republic of Korea) |
| Bronze | Yasniel Toledo Lopez (Cuba) |
| Bronze | Evaldas Petrauskas (Lithuania) |

### Men's Light Welter Weight (64kg)
| | |
|---|---|
| Gold | Roniel Sotolongo (Cuba) |
| Silver | Denys Berinchyk (Ukraine) |
| Bronze | Vincenzo Mangiacapre (Italy) |
| Bronze | Munkh-Erdene Uranchimeg (Mongolia) |

### Men's Welter Weight (69kg)
| | |
|---|---|
| Gold | Serik Sapiyev (Kazakhstan) |
| Silver | Freddie Evans (GBR) |
| Bronze | Andrey Zamkovoy (Russian Fed.) |
| Bronze | Taras Shelestyuk (Ukraine) |

### Men's Middle Weight (75kg)
| | |
|---|---|
| Gold | Ryota Murata (Japan) |
| Silver | Esquiva Falcao Florentino (Brazil) |
| Bronze | Anthony Ogogo (GBR) |
| Bronze | Ryota Murata (Japan) |

### Men's Light Heavy Weight (81kg)
| | |
|---|---|
| Gold | Egor Mekhontcev (Russian Fed.) |
| Silver | Adilbek Niyazymbetov (Kazakhstan) |
| Bronze | Yamaguchi Falcao Florentino (Brazil) |
| Bronze | Oleksandr Gvozdyk (Ukraine) |

Boxing Middle Weight champion Ryota Murata

### Men's Heavy Weight (91kg)
| | |
|---|---|
| Gold | Oleksandr Usyk (Ukraine) |
| Silver | Clemente Russo (Italy) |
| Bronze | Tervel Pulev (Bulgaria) |
| Bronze | Teymur Mammadov (Azerbaijan) |

### Men's Super Heavy Weight (+91kg)
| | |
|---|---|
| Gold | Anthony Joshua (GBR) |
| Silver | Roberto Cammarelle (Italy) |
| Bronze | Ivan Dychko (Kazakhstan) |
| Bronze | Magomedrasul Medzhidov (Azerbaijan) |

### Women's Fly Weight (51kg)
| | |
|---|---|
| Gold | Nicola Adams (GBR) |
| Silver | Cancan Ren (China) |
| Bronze | Marlen Esparza (USA) |
| Bronze | Mary Kom (India) |

### Women's Light Weight (60kg)
| | |
|---|---|
| Gold | Katie Taylor (Ireland) |
| Silver | Sofya Ochigava (Russian Fed.) |
| Bronze | Mavzuna Chorieva (Tajikistan) |
| Bronze | Adriana Araujo (Brazil) |

### Women's Middle Weight (75kg)
| | |
|---|---|
| Gold | Claressa Shields (USA) |
| Silver | Nadezda Torlopova (Russian Fed.) |
| Bronze | Marina Volnova (Kazakhstan) |
| Bronze | Jinzi Li (China) |

## Canoe Slalom

### Men's Canoe Single (C1)
| | | |
|---|---|---|
| Gold | Tony Estanguet (France) | 97.06 |
| Silver | Sideris Tasiadis (Germany) | 98.09 |
| Bronze | Michal Martikan (Slovakia) | 98.31 |

### Men's Canoe Double (C2)
| | | |
|---|---|---|
| Gold | Great Britain | 106.41 |
| | (Tim Baillie, Etienne Stott) | |
| Silver | Great Britain | 106.77 |
| | (David Florence, Richard Hounslow) | |
| Bronze | Slovakia | 108.28 |
| | (Peter Hochschorner, Pavol Hochschorner) | |

### Men's Kayak (K1)
| | | |
|---|---|---|
| Gold | Daniele Molmenti (Italy) | 93.43 |
| Silver | Vavrinec Hradilek (Czech Rep) | 94.78 |
| Bronze | Hannes Aigner (Germany) | 94.92 |

### Women's Kayak (K1)
| | | |
|---|---|---|
| Gold | Emilie Fer (France) | 105.90 |
| Silver | Jessica Fox (Australia) | 106.51 |
| Bronze | Maialen Chourraut (Spain) | 106.87 |

# Event results

## Canoe Sprint

**Men's Kayak Single (K1) 1000m**
| | | |
|---|---|---|
| Gold | Eirik Larsen (Norway) | 3:26.462 |
| Silver | Adam Van Koeverden (Canada) | 3:27.170 |
| Bronze | Max Hoff (Germany) | 3:27.759 |

**Men's Kayak Single (K1) 200m**
| | | |
|---|---|---|
| Gold | Ed McKeever (GBR) | 36.246 |
| Silver | Saul Rivero (Spain) | 36.540 |
| Bronze | Mark De Jonge (Canada) | 36.657 |

**Men's Kayak Double (K2) 1000m**
| | | |
|---|---|---|
| Gold | Hungary | 3:09.646 |
| | (Rudolf Dombi, Roland Kokeny) | |
| Silver | Portugal | 3:09.699 |
| | Fernando Pimenta, Emanuel Silva) | |
| Bronze | Germany | 3:10.117 |
| | (Martin Hollstein, Andreas Ihle) | |

**Men's Kayak Double (K2) 200m**
| | | |
|---|---|---|
| Gold | Russian Fed | 33.507 |
| | (Yury Postigay, Alexander Dyachenko) | |
| Silver | Belarus | 34.266 |
| | (Raman Piatrushenka, Vadzim Makhneu) | |
| Bronze | Great Britain | 34.421 |
| | (Liam Heath, Jon Schofield) | |

**Men's Kayak Four (K4) 1000m**
| | | |
|---|---|---|
| Gold | Australia | 2:55.085 |
| Silver | Hungary | 2:55.699 |
| Bronze | Czech Republic | 2:55.850 |

**Men's Canoe Single (C1)1000m**
| | | |
|---|---|---|
| Gold | Sebastian Brendel (Germany) | 3:47.176 |
| Silver | David Cal Figueroa (Spain) | 3:48.053 |
| Bronze | Mark Oldershaw (Canada) | 3:48.502 |

**Men's Canoe Single (C1) 200m**
| | | |
|---|---|---|
| Gold | Yuri Cheban (Ukraine) | 42.291 |
| Silver | Jevgenij Shuklin (Lithuania) | 42.792 |
| Bronze | Ivan Shtyl (Russian Fed.) | 42.853 |

**Men's Canoe Double (C2) 1000m**
| | | |
|---|---|---|
| Gold | Germany | 3:33.804 |
| | (Peter Kretschmer, Kurt Kuschela) | |
| Silver | Belarus | 3:35.206 |
| | (Andrei Bahdonovich, Aliaksandr Bahdonovic) | |
| Bronze | Russian Fed | 3:36.414 |
| | (Alexey Korovashkov, Ilya Pervukhin) | |

**Women's Kayak Single (K1) 500m**
| | | |
|---|---|---|
| Gold | Danuta Kozak (Hungary) | 1:51.456 |
| Silver | Inna Osypenko-Radomska (Ukraine) | 1:52.685 |
| Bronze | Bridgitte Hartley (S Africa) | 1:52.923 |

**Women's Kayak Double (K2) 500m**
| | | |
|---|---|---|
| Gold | Germany | 1:42.213 |
| | (Franziska Weber, Tina Dietze) | |
| Silver | Hungary | 1:43.278 |
| | (Katalin, Kovacs, Natasa Douchev-Janics) | |
| Bronze | Poland | 1:44.000 |
| | (Koralina Naja, Beata Mikolajczyk) | |

**0Women's Kayak Four (K4) 500m**
| | | |
|---|---|---|
| Gold | Hungary | 1:30.827 |
| Silver | Germany | 1:31.298 |
| Bronze | Belarus | 1:31.400 |

**Women's Kayak Single (K1) 200m**
| | | |
|---|---|---|
| Gold | Lisa Carrington (New Zealand) | 44.638 |
| Silver | Inna Osypenko-Radomska (Ukraine) | 45.053 |
| Bronze | Natasa Douchev-Janics (Hungary) | 45.128 |

## Cycling — BMX

**Men**
| | | |
|---|---|---|
| Gold | Maris Strombergs (Latvia) | 37.576 |
| Silver | Sam Willoughby (Australia) | 37.929 |
| Bronze | Carlos Zabala (Colombia) | 38.251 |

**Women**
| | | |
|---|---|---|
| Gold | Mariana Pajon (Colombia) | 37.706 |
| Silver | Sarah Walker (New Zealand) | 38.133 |
| Bronze | Laura Smulders (Netherlands) | 38.231 |

## Cycling — Mountain Bike

**Men's Cross-Country**
| | | |
|---|---|---|
| Gold | Jaroslav Kulhavy (Czech Rep) | 1:29:7 |
| Silver | Nino Schurter (Switzerland) | 1:29:08 |
| Bronze | Marco Aurelio Fontana (Italy) | 1:29:32 |

**Women's Cross-Country**
| | | |
|---|---|---|
| Gold | Julie Bresset (France) | 1:30:52 |
| Silver | Sabine Spitz (Germany) | 1:31:54 |
| Bronze | Georgia Gould (USA) | 1:32:00 |

## Cycling — Road

**Men's Road Race**
| | | |
|---|---|---|
| Gold | Alexandr Vinokurov (Kazakhstan) | 5:45:57 |
| Silver | Rigoberto Uran (Colombia) | 5:45:57 |
| Bronze | Alexander Kristoff (Norway) | 5:46:05 |

**Men's Time Trial**
| | | |
|---|---|---|
| Gold | Bradley Wiggins (GBR) | 50:39.54 |
| Silver | Tony Martin (Germany) | 51:21.54 |
| Bronze | Christopher Froome (GBR) | 51:47.87 |

**Women's Road Race**
| | | |
|---|---|---|
| Gold | Marianne Vos (Netherlands) | 3:35:29 |
| Silver | Elizabeth Armitstead (GBR) | 3:35:29 |
| Bronze | Olga Zabelinskaya (Russian Fed.) | 3:35:31 |

**Women's Time Trial**
| | | |
|---|---|---|
| Gold | Kristin Armstrong (USA) | 37:34.82 |
| Silver | Judith Arndt (Germany) | 37:50.29 |
| Bronze | Olga Zabelinskaya (Russian Fed.) | 37:57.35 |

## Cycling — Track

**Men's Sprint**
| | | |
|---|---|---|
| Gold | Jason Kenny (GBR) | |
| Silver | Gregory Bauge (France) | |
| Bronze | Shane Perkins (Australia) | |

**Men's Keirin**
| | | |
|---|---|---|
| Gold | Chris Hoy (GBR) | |
| Silver | Maximilian Levy (Germany) | |
| Bronze | Simon Van Velthooven (New Zealand) | |

**Men's Team Sprint**
| | | |
|---|---|---|
| Gold | Great Britain | 42.600 [WR] |
| | (Philip Hindes, Chris Hoy, Jason Kenny) | |
| Silver | France | 43.013 |
| | (Gregory Bauge, Michael D'Almeida, Kevin Sireau) | |
| Bronze | Germany | 43.209 |
| | (Rene Enders, Robert Forstemann, Max Levy) | |

**Men's Team Pursuit**
| | | |
|---|---|---|
| Gold | Great Britain | 3:51.659 [WR] |
| | (Ed Clancy, Geraint Thomas, Peter Kennaugh, Steven Burke) | |
| Silver | Australia | 3:54.581 |
| | (Jack Bobridge, Glenn O'Shea, Rohan Dennis, Michael Hepburn) | |
| Bronze | New Zealand | 3:55.952 |
| | (Sam Bewley, Marc Ryan, Jesse Sergent, Aaron Gate) | |

**Men's Omnium**
| | | |
|---|---|---|
| Gold | Lasse Norman Hansen (Denmark) | 27 |
| Silver | Bryan Coquard (France) | 29 |
| Bronze | Ed Clancy (GBR) | 30 |

**Women's Sprint**
| | | |
|---|---|---|
| Gold | Anna Meares (Australia) | |
| Silver | Victoria Pendleton (GBR) | |
| Bronze | Shuang Guo (China) | |

**Women's Keirin**
| | | |
|---|---|---|
| Gold | Victoria Pendleton (GBR) | |
| Silver | Shuang Guo (China) | |
| Bronze | Wai Sze Lee (Hong Kong) | |

**Women's Team Sprint**
| | | |
|---|---|---|
| Gold | Germany | 32.798 |
| | (Miriam Welt, Kristina Vogel) | |
| Silver | China (relegated) | 32.619 |
| | (Gong Jinji, Guo Shuang) | |
| Bronze | Australia | 32.727 |
| | (Anna Meares, Karle McCulloch) | |

**Women's Team Pursuit**
| | | |
|---|---|---|
| Gold | Great Britain | 3:14.051 [WR] |
| | (Joanna Rowsell, Dani King, Laura Trott) | |
| Silver | United States | 3:19.727 |
| | (Sarah Hammer, Dotsie Bausch, Jennie Reed) | |
| Bronze | Canada | 3:17.915 |
| | (Tara Whitten, Gillian Carleton, Jasmin Glaesser) | |

**Women's Omnium**
| | | |
|---|---|---|
| Gold | Laura Trott (GBR) | 18 |
| Silver | Sarah Hammer (USA) | 19 |
| Bronze | Annette Edmondson (Australia) | 24 |

## Diving

**Men's 3m Springboard**
| | | |
|---|---|---|
| Gold | Ilya Zakharov (Russian Fed.) | 555.90 |
| Silver | Kai Qin (China) | 541.75 |
| Bronze | Chong He (China) | 524.15 |

**Men's 10m Platform**
| | | |
|---|---|---|
| Gold | David Boudia (USA) | 568.65 |
| Silver | Bo Qiu (China) | 566.85 |
| Bronze | Tom Daley (GBR) | 556.95 |

**Men's Synchronised 3m Springboard**
| | | |
|---|---|---|
| Gold | China | 477.00 |
| | (Yutong Luo, Kai Qin) | |
| Silver | Russian Federation | 459.63 |
| | (Ilya Zakharov, Evgeny Kuznetsov) | |
| Bronze | United States | 446.70 |
| | (Troy Dumais, Kristian Ipsen) | |

**Men's Synchronised 10m Platform**
| | | |
|---|---|---|
| Gold | China | 486.78 |
| | (Yuan Cao, Yangquan Zhang) | |
| Silver | Mexico | 468.90 |
| | (Ivan Navarro Garcia, German Sanchez) | |
| Bronze | United States | 463.47 |
| | (David Boudia, Nicholas McCrory) | |

**Women's 3m Springboard**
| | | |
|---|---|---|
| Gold | Minxia Wu (China) | 414 |
| Silver | Zi He (China) | 379.20 |
| Bronze | Laura Sanchez Soto (Mexico) | 362.40 |

Great Britain won seven of the 10 Track Cycling events

**Women's 10m Platform**

| | | |
|---|---|---|
| Gold | Ruoling Chen (China) | 422.30 |
| Silver | Brittany Broben (Australia) | 366.50 |
| Bronze | Pandelela Pamg (Malaysia) | 359.20 |

**Women's Synchronised 3m Springboard**

| | | |
|---|---|---|
| Gold | China | 346.20 |
| | (Minxia Wu, Zi He) | |
| Silver | United States | 321.90 |
| | (Kelci Bryant, Abigail Johnston) | |
| Bronze | Canada | 316.80 |
| | (Jennifer Abel, Emilie Heymans) | |

**Women's Synchronised 10m Platform**

| | | |
|---|---|---|
| Gold | China (Ruolin Chen, Hao Wang) | 368.40 |
| Silver | Mexico | 343.32 |
| | (Paola Sanchez, Alejandra Loza) | |
| Bronze | Canada | 337.62 |
| | (Meaghan Benfeito, Roseline Filion) | |

## Equestrian

**Dressage Individual**

| | | |
|---|---|---|
| Gold | Charlotte Dujardin (GBR) | 90.089 |
| Silver | Adelinde Cornelissen (Netherlands) | 88.196 |
| Bronze | Laura Bechtolsheimer (GBR) | 84.339 |

**Dressage Team**

| | | |
|---|---|---|
| Gold | Great Britain | 79.979 |
| Silver | Germany | 78.216 |
| Bronze | Netherlands | 77.124 |

**Jumping Individual**

| | | |
|---|---|---|
| Gold | Steve Guerdat (Switzerland) | 0 |
| Silver | Gerco Schroder (Netherlands) | 1 |
| Bronze | Cian O'Connor (Ireland) | 1 |

**Jumping Team**

| | | |
|---|---|---|
| Gold | Great Britain | 4 |
| Silver | Netherlands | 4 |
| Bronze | Saudi Arabia | 13 |

**Eventing Individual**

| | | |
|---|---|---|
| Gold | Michael Jung (Germany) | 40.60 |
| Silver | Sara Algotsson Ostholt (Sweden) | 43.30 |
| Bronze | Sandra Auffarth (Germany) | 44.80 |

**Eventing Team**

| | | |
|---|---|---|
| Gold | Germany | 133.70 |
| Silver | Great Britain | 138.20 |
| Bronze | New Zealand | 144.40 |

## Fencing

**Men's Individual Foil**

| | |
|---|---|
| Gold | Sheng Lei (China) |
| Silver | Alaaeldin Abouelkassem (Egypt) |
| Bronze | Byungchul Choi (Republic of Korea) |

**Women's Individual Foil**

| | |
|---|---|
| Gold | Elisa Di Francisca (Italy) |
| Silver | Arianna Errigo (Italy) |
| Bronze | Valentina Vezzali (Italy) |

**Men's Individual Epée**

| | |
|---|---|
| Gold | Ruben Limardo Gascon (Venezuela) |
| Silver | Bartosz Piasecki (Norway) |
| Bronze | Jinsun Jung (Republic of Korea) |

**Women's Individual Epée**

| | |
|---|---|
| Gold | Yana Shemyakina (Ukraine) |
| Silver | Britta Heidemann (Germany) |
| Bronze | Yujie Sun (China) |

**Men's Individual Sabre**

| | |
|---|---|
| Gold | Aron Szilagyi (Hungary) |
| Silver | Diego Occhiuzzi (Italy) |
| Bronze | Nikolay Kovalev (Russian Fed.) |

**Women's Individual Sabre**

| | |
|---|---|
| Gold | Jiyeon Kim (Republic of Korea) |
| Silver | Sofya Velikaya (Russian Fed.) |
| Bronze | Olga Kharlan (Ukraine) |

**Men's Foil Team**

| | |
|---|---|
| Gold | Italy |
| Silver | Japan |
| Bronze | Germany |

**Women's Foil Team**

| | |
|---|---|
| Gold | Italy |
| Silver | Russian Federation |
| Bronze | Republic of Korea |

**Men's Team Sabre**

| | |
|---|---|
| Gold | Korea |
| Silver | Romania |
| Bronze | Italy |

**Women's Epée Team**

| | |
|---|---|
| Gold | China |
| Silver | Republic of Korea |
| Bronze | United States |

## Football

**Men**

| | |
|---|---|
| Gold | Mexico |
| Silver | Brazil |
| Bronze | Republic of Korea |

**Women**

| | |
|---|---|
| Gold | United States |
| Silver | Japan |
| Bronze | Canada |

## Gymnastics — Artistic

**Men's Individual All-Around**

| | | |
|---|---|---|
| Gold | Kohei Uchimura (Japan) | 92.690 |
| Silver | Marcel Nguyen (Germany) | 91.031 |
| Bronze | Danell Leyva (USA) | 90.698 |

**Men's Floor Exercise**

| | | |
|---|---|---|
| Gold | Kai Zou (China) | 15.933 |
| Silver | Kohei Uchimura (Japan) | 15.800 |
| Silver | Denis Ablyazin (Russian Fed.) | 15.800 |

**Men's Pommel Horse**

| | | |
|---|---|---|
| Gold | Krisztian Berki (Hungary) | 16.066 |
| Silver | Louis Smith (GBR) | 16.066 |
| Bronze | Max Whitlock (GBR) | 15.600 |

**Men's Rings**

| | | |
|---|---|---|
| Gold | Arthur Zanetti (Brazil) | 15.900 |
| Silver | Yibing Chen (China) | 15.800 |
| Bronze | Matteo Morandi (Italy) | 15.733 |

**Men's Vault**

| | | |
|---|---|---|
| Gold | Hak Seon Yang (Rep Korea) | 16.533 |
| Silver | Denis Ablyazin (Russian Fed.) | 16.399 |
| Bronze | Igor Radivilov (Ukraine) | 16.316 |

**Men's Parallel Bars**

| | | |
|---|---|---|
| Gold | Zhe Feng (China) | 15.966 |
| Silver | Marcel Nguyen (Germany) | 15.800 |
| Bronze | Hamilton Sabot (France) | 15.566 |

**Men's Horizontal Bar**

| | | |
|---|---|---|
| Gold | Epke Zonderland (Netherlands) | 16.533 |
| Silver | Fabian Hambuchen (Germany) | 16.400 |
| Bronze | Kai Zou (China) | 16.366 |

**Men's Team**

| | | |
|---|---|---|
| Gold | China | 275.997 |
| Silver | Japan | 271.952 |
| Bronze | Great Britain | 271.711 |

**Women's Individual All-Around**

| | | |
|---|---|---|
| Gold | Gabrielle Douglas (USA) | 62.232 |
| Silver | Victoria Komova (Russian Fed.) | 61.973 |
| Bronze | Aliya Mustafina (Russian Fed.) | 59.566 |

**Women's Vault**

| | | |
|---|---|---|
| Gold | Sandra Izbasa (Romania) | 15.191 |
| Silver | Mc Kayla Maroney (USA) | 15.083 |
| Bronze | Maria Paseka (Russian Fed.) | 15.050 |

**Women's Uneven Bars**

| | | |
|---|---|---|
| Gold | Aliya Mustafina (Russian Fed.) | 16.133 |
| Silver | Kexin He (China) | 15.933 |
| Bronze | Beth Tweddle (GBR) | 15.916 |

**Women's Beam**

| | | |
|---|---|---|
| Gold | Linlin Deng (China) | 15.600 |
| Silver | Lu Swi (China) | 15.500 |
| Bronze | Alexandra Raisman (USA) | 15.066 |

**Women's Floor Exercise**

| | | |
|---|---|---|
| Gold | Alexandra Raisman (USA) | 15.600 |
| Silver | Catalina Ponor (Romania) | 15.200 |
| Bronze | Aliya Mustafina (Russian Fed.) | 14.900 |

**Women's Team**

| | | |
|---|---|---|
| Gold | United States | 183.596 |
| Silver | Russian Fed | 178.530 |
| Bronze | Romania | 176.414 |

## Gymnastics — Rhythmic

**Individual All-Around Competition**

| | | |
|---|---|---|
| Gold | Evgeniya Kanaeva (Russian Fed.) | 116.900 |
| Silver | Daria Dmitrieva (Russian Fed.) | 114.500 |
| Bronze | Liubou Charkashyna (Bulgaria) | 111.700 |

**Group All-Around Final**

| | | |
|---|---|---|
| Gold | Russian Federation | 57.000 |
| Silver | Belarus | 55.500 |
| Bronze | Italy | 55.450 |

## Gymnastics — Trampoline

**Men**

| | | |
|---|---|---|
| Gold | Dong Dong (China) | 62.990 |
| Silver | Dmitry Ushakov (Russian Fed.) | 61.769 |
| Bronze | Chunlong Lu (China) | 61.319 |

**Women**

| | | |
|---|---|---|
| Gold | Rosannagh Maclennan (Canada) | 57.305 |
| Silver | Shanshan Huang (China) | 56.730 |
| Bronze | Wenna He (China) | 55.950 |

## Handball

**Men**

| | |
|---|---|
| Gold | France |
| Silver | Sweden |
| Bronze | Croatia |

**Women**

| | |
|---|---|
| Gold | Norway |
| Silver | Montenegro |
| Bronze | Spain |

## Hockey

**Men**

| | |
|---|---|
| Gold | Germany |
| Silver | Netherlands |
| Bronze | Australia |

**Women**

| | |
|---|---|
| Gold | Netherlands |
| Silver | Argentina |
| Bronze | Great Britain |

# Event results

## Judo

**Men's Extra Lightweight (-60kg)**
Gold — Arsen Galstyan (Russian Fed.)
Silver — Hiroaki Hiraoka (Japan)
Bronze — Rishod Sobirov (Uzbekistan)
Bronze — Felipe Kitadai (Brazil)

**Men's Half-Lightweight (-66kg)**
Gold — Lasha Shavdatuashvili (Georgia)
Silver — Miklos Ungvari (Hungary)
Bronze — Masashi Ebinuma (Japan)
Bronze — Jun-Ho Cho (Republic of Korea)

**Men's Lightweight (-73 kg)**
Gold — Mansur Isaev (Russian Fed.)
Silver — Riki Nakaya (Japan)
Bronze — Nyam-Ochir Sainjargal (Mongolia)
Bronze — Ugo Legrand (France)

**Men's Half-Middleweight (-81kg)**
Gold — Jae-Bum Kim (Republic of Korea)
Silver — Ole Bischof (Germany)
Bronze — Ivan Nifontov (Russian Fed.)
Bronze — Antoine Valois-Fortier (Canada)

**Men's Middleweight (-90kg)**
Gold — Dae Nam Song (Republic of Korea)
Silver — Asley Gonzalez (Cuba)
Bronze — Ilias Iliadis (Greece)
Bronze — Masashi Nishiyama (Japan)

**Men's Half-Heavyweight (-100kg)**
Gold — Tagir Khaibulaev (Russian Fed.)
Silver — Tuvshinbayar Naidan (Mongolia)
Bronze — Dimitri Peters (Germany)
Bronze — Henk Grol (Netherlands)

**Men's Heavyweight (+100kg)**
Gold — Teddy Riner (France)
Silver — Alexander Mikhaylin (Russian Fed.)
Bronze — Andreas Toelzer (Germany)
Bronze — Rafael Silva (Brazil)

**Women's Extra Lightweight (-48kg)**
Gold — Sarah Menezes (Brazil)
Silver — Alina Dumitru (Romania)
Bronze — Charline Van Snick (Belgium)
Bronze — Eva Csernoviczki (Hungary)

**Women's Half-Lightweight (-52kg)**
Gold — Kum Ae An (DPR Korea)
Silver — Yanet Bermoy Acosta (Cuba)
Bronze — Rosalba Forciniti (Italy)
Bronze — Priscilla Gneto (France)

**Women's Lightweight (-57kg)**
Gold — Kaori Matsumoto (Japan)
Silver — Corina Caprioriu (Romania)
Bronze — Marti Malloy (USA)
Bronze — Automne Pavia (France)

**Women's Half Middleweight (-63kg)**
Gold — Urska Zolnir (Slovenia)
Silver — Lili Xu (China)
Bronze — Yoshie Ueno (Japan)
Bronze — Gevrise Emane (France)

**Women's Half-Heavyweight (-78kg)**
Gold — Kayla Harrison (USA)
Silver — Gemma Gibbons (GBR)
Bronze — Audrey Tcheumeo (France)
Bronze — Mayra Aguiar (Brazil)

**Women's Heavyweight (+78kg)**
Gold — Idalys Ortiz (Cuba)
Silver — Mika Sugimoto (Japan)
Bronze — Karina Bryant (GBR)
Bronze — Wen Tong (China)

## Modern Pentathlon

**Men**
Gold — David Svoboda (Czech Republic) 5928
Silver — Zhongrong Cao (China) 5904
Bronze — Adam Marosi (Hungary) 5836

**Women**
Gold — Laura Asadauskaite (Lithuania) 5356
Silver — Samantha Murray (GBR) 5356
Bronze — Yane Marques (Brazil) 5340

## Rowing

**Men's Single Sculls**
Gold — Mahe Drysdale (New Zealand) 6:57.82
Silver — Ondrej Synek (Czech Rep) 6:59.37
Bronze — Alan Campbell (GBR) 7:03.28

**Men's Pair**
Gold — New Zealand 6:16.65
(Eric Murray, Hamish Bond)
Silver — France 6:21.11
(Germain Chardin, Dorian Mortelette)
Bronze — Great Britain 6:21.77
(George Nash, William Satch)

**Men's Double Sculls**
Gold — New Zealand 6:31.67
(Nathan Cohen, Joseph Sullivan)
Silver — Italy 6:32.80
(Alessio Sartori, Romano Battisti)
Bronze — Slovenia 6:34.35
(Luka Skip, Iztok Cop)

**Men's Four**
Gold — Great Britain 6:3.97
Silver — Australia 6:05.19
Bronze — United States 6:07.20

**Men's Quadruple Sculls**
Gold — Germany 5:42.48
Silver — Croatia 5:44.78
Bronze — Australia 5:45.22

**Men's Eight**
Gold — Germany 5:48.75
Silver — Canada 5:49.98
Bronze — Great Britain 5:51.18

**Men's Lightweight Double Sculls**
Gold — Denmark 6:37.17
(Mads Rasmussen, Rasmus Quist)
Silver — Great Britain 6:37.78
(Zac Purchase, Mark Hunter)
Bronze — New Zealand 6:40.86
(Storm Uru, Peter Taylor)

**Men's Lightweight Four**
Gold — South Africa 6:02.84
Silver — Great Britain 6:03.09
Bronze — Denmark 6:03.16

Rowing Single Sculls champion Mahe Drysdale

**Women's Single Sculls**
Gold — Miroslava Knapkova (Czech Rep) 7:54.37
Silver — Fie Udby Erichsen (Denmark) 7:57.72
Bronze — Kim Crow (Australia) 7:58.04

**Women's Pair**
Gold — Great Britain 7:27.13
(Helen Glover, Heather Stanning)
Silver — Australia 7:29.86
(Kate Hornsey, Sarah Tait)
Bronze — New Zealand 7:30.19
(Juliette Haigh, Rebecca Scown)

**Women's Double Sculls**
Gold — Great Britain 6:55.82
(Katherine Grainger, Anna Watkins)
Silver — Australia 6:58.55
(Kim Crow, Brooke Pratley)
Bronze — Poland 7:07.92
(Magdalena Fularczyk, Julia Michalska)

**Women's Quadruple Sculls**
Gold — Ukraine 6:35.93
Silver — Germany 6:38.09
Bronze — United States 6:40.63

**Women's Eight**
Gold — United States 6:10.59
Silver — Canada 6:12.06
Bronze — Netherlands 6:13.12

**Women's Lightweight Double Sculls**
Gold — Great Britain 7:9.30
(Katherine Copeland, Sophie Hosking)
Silver — China 7:11.93
(Dongxiang Xu, Wenyi Huang)
Bronze — Greece 7:12.09
(Christina Giazitzidou, Alexandra Tsiavou)

## Sailing

**Men's RS:X**
Gold — Dorian Van Rijsselberge (Netherlands) 15
Silver — Nick Dempsey (GBR) 41
Bronze — Przemyslaw Miarczynski (Poland) 60

**Men's Laser**
Gold — Tom Slingsby (Australia)
Silver — Pavlos Kontides (Cyprus)
Bronze — Rasmus Myrgren (Sweden)

**Men's Finn**
Gold — Ben Ainslie (GBR) 46
Silver — Jonas Høgh-Christensen (Denmark) 46
Bronze — Jonathan Lobert (France) 49

**Men's 470**
Gold — Australia 22
(Mathew Belcher, Malcolm Page)
Silver — Great Britain 30
(Luke Patience, Stuart Bithell)
Bronze — Argentina 63
(Lucas Calabrese, Juan de la Fuente)

**Men's 49er**
Gold — Australia 56
(Nathan Outteridge, Iain Jensen)
Silver — New Zealand 80
(Peter Burling, Blair Tuke)
Bronze — Denmark 114
(Allan Norregaard, Peter Lang)

**Men's Star**
Gold — Sweden 32
(Fredrik Loof, Max Salminen)
Silver — Great Britain 34
(Iain Percy, Andrew Simpson)
Bronze — Brazil 40
(Robert Scheidt, Bruno Prada)

**Women's RS:X**
| | | |
|---|---|---|
| Gold | Marina Alabau Neira (Spain) | 26 |
| Silver | Tuuli Petaja (Finland) | 46 |
| Bronze | Zofia Noceti-Klepacka (Poland) | 47 |

**Women's Laser Radial**
| | |
|---|---|
| Gold | Lijia Xu (China) |
| Silver | Marit Bouwmeester (Netherlands) |
| Bronze | Evi Van Acker (Belgium) |

**Women's 470**
| | | |
|---|---|---|
| Gold | New Zealand | 35 |
| | (Jo Aleh, Olivia Powrie) | |
| Silver | Great Britain | 51 |
| | (Hannah Mills, Saskia Clark) | |
| Bronze | Netherlands | 64 |
| | (Lisa Westerhof, Lobke Berkhout) | |

**Women's Elliott 6m**
| | |
|---|---|
| Gold | Spain |
| Silver | Australia |
| Bronze | Finland |

## Shooting

**Men's 50m Rifle 3 Positions**
| | | |
|---|---|---|
| Golf | Niccolo Campriani (Italy) | 1278.5 [OR] |
| Silver | Jonghyun Kim (Rep Korea) | 1272.5 |
| Bronze | Matthew Emmons (USA) | 1271.3 |

**Men's 50m Rifle Prone**
| | | |
|---|---|---|
| Gold | Sergei Martynov (Bulgaria) | 705.5 [WR] |
| Silver | Lionel Cox (Belgium) | 701.5 |
| Bronze | Rajmond Debevec (Slovenia) | 701.0 |

**Men's 10m Air Rifle**
| | | |
|---|---|---|
| Gold | Alin George Moldoveanu (Romania) | 702.1 |
| Silver | Niccolo Campriani (Italy) | 701.5 |
| Bronze | Gagan Narang (India) | 701.1 |

**Men's 50m Pistol**
| | | |
|---|---|---|
| Gold | Jongoh Jin (Rep Korea) | 662.0 |
| Silver | Young Rae Choi (Rep Korea) | 661.5 |
| Bronze | Zhiwei Wang (China) | 658.6 |

**Men's 25m Rapid Fire Pistol**
| | | |
|---|---|---|
| Gold | Leuris Pupo (Cuba) | 34 |
| Silver | Vijay Kumar (India) | 30 |
| Bronze | Feng Ding (China) | 27 |

**Men's 10m Air Pistol**
| | | |
|---|---|---|
| Gold | Jin Jong Oh (Rep Korea) | 688.2 |
| Silver | Luca Tesconi (Italy) | 685.8 |
| Bronze | Andrija Zlatic (Serbia) | 685.2 |

**Men's Trap**
| | | |
|---|---|---|
| Gold | Giovanni Cernogoraz (Croatia) | 146 [OR] |
| Silver | Massimo Fabbrizi (Italy) | 146 [OR] |
| Bronze | Fehaid Aldeehani (Kuwait) | 145 |

**Men's Double Trap**
| | | |
|---|---|---|
| Gold | Peter Wilson (GBR) | 188 |
| Silver | Hakan Dahlby (Sweden) | 186 |
| Bronze | Vasily Mosin (Russian Fed.) | 185 |

**Men's Skeet**
| | | |
|---|---|---|
| Gold | Vincent Hancock (USA) | 148 [OR] |
| Silver | Anders Golding (Denmark) | 146 |
| Bronze | Nasser Al-Attiya (Qatar) | 144 |

**Women's 10m Air Rifle**
| | | |
|---|---|---|
| Gold | Siling Yi (China) | 502.9 |
| Silver | Sylwia Bogacka (Poland) | 502.2 |
| Bronze | Dan Yu (China) | 501.5 |

**Women's 50m Rifle 3 Positions**
| | | |
|---|---|---|
| Gold | Jamie Lynn Gray (USA) | 691.9 [OR] |
| Silver | Ivana Maksimovic (Serbia) | 687.5 |
| Bronze | Adela Sykorova (Czech Rep) | 683.0 |

The women's 10m Air Rifle Victory Ceremony

**Women's 25m Pistol**
| | | |
|---|---|---|
| Gold | Jangmi Kim (Republic of Korea) | 792.4 |
| Silver | Ying Chen (China) | 791.4 |
| Bronze | Olena Kostevych (Ukraine) | 788.6 |

**Women's 10m Air Pistol**
| | | |
|---|---|---|
| Gold | Wenjun Guo (China) | 488.1 |
| Silver | Celine Goberville (France) | 486.6 |
| Bronze | Olena Kostevych (Ukraine) | 486.6 |

**Women's Trap**
| | | |
|---|---|---|
| Gold | Jessica Rossi (Italy) | 99 [WR] |
| Silver | Zuzana Stefecekova (Slovakia) | 93 |
| Bronze | Delphine Reau (France) | 93 |

**Women's Skeet**
| | | |
|---|---|---|
| Gold | Kimberly Rhode (USA) | 99 [OR] |
| Silver | Ning Wei (China) | 91 |
| Bronze | Danka Bartekova (Slovakia) | 90 |

## Swimming

**Men's 50m Freestyle**
| | | |
|---|---|---|
| Gold | Florent Manaudou (France) | 21.34 |
| Silver | Cullen Jones (USA) | 21.54 |
| Bronze | Cesar Cielo (Brazil) | 21.59 |

**Men's 100m Freestyle**
| | | |
|---|---|---|
| Gold | Nathan Adrian (USA) | 47.52 |
| Silver | James Magnussen (Australia) | 47.53 |
| Bronze | Brent Hayden (Canada) | 47.80 |

**Men's 200m Freestyle**
| | | |
|---|---|---|
| Gold | Yannick Agnel (France) | 1:43.14 |
| Silver | Taehwan Park (Rep Korea) | 1:44.93 |
| Silver | Yang Sun (China) | 1:44.93 |

**Men's 400m Freestyle**
| | | |
|---|---|---|
| Gold | Sun Yang (China) | 3:40.14 [OR] |
| Silver | Park Taehwan (Rep Korea) | 3:42.06 |
| Bronze | Peter Vanderkaay (USA) | 3:44.69 |

**Men's 1500m Freestyle**
| | | |
|---|---|---|
| Gold | Yang Sun (China) | 14:31.02 [WR] |
| Silver | Ryan Cochrane (Canada) | 14:39.63 |
| Bronze | Oussama Mellouli (Tunisia) | 14:40.31 |

**Men's 100m Backstroke**
| | | |
|---|---|---|
| Gold | Matthew Grevers (USA) | 52.16 [OR] |
| Silver | Nick Thoman (USA) | 52.92 |
| Bronze | Ryosuke Irie (Japan) | 52.97 |

**Men's 200m Backstroke**
| | | |
|---|---|---|
| Gold | Tyler Clary (USA) | 1:53.41 [OR] |
| Silver | Ryosuke Irie (Japan) | 1:53.78 |
| Bronze | Ryan Lochte (USA) | 1:53.94 |

**Men's 100m Breaststroke**
| | | |
|---|---|---|
| Gold | Cameron Van Der Burgh (S Africa) | 58.46 [WR] |
| Silver | Christian Sprenger (Australia) | 58.93 |
| Bronze | Brendan Hansen (USA) | 59.49 |

**Men's 200m Breaststroke**
| | | |
|---|---|---|
| Gold | Daniel Gyurta (Hungary) | 2:07.28 [WR] |
| Silver | Michael Jamieson (GBR) | 2:07.43 |
| Bronze | Ryo Tateishi (Japan) | 2:08.29 |

**Men's 100m Butterfly**
| | | |
|---|---|---|
| Gold | Michael Phelps (USA) | 51.21 |
| Silver | Chad Le Clos (South Africa) | 51.44 |
| Silver | Evgeny Korotyshkin (Russian Fed.) | 51.44 |

**Men's 200m Butterfly**
| | | |
|---|---|---|
| Gold | Chad Le Clos (South Africa) | 1:52.96 |
| Silver | Michael Phelps (USA) | 1:53.01 |
| Bronze | Takeshi Matsuda (Japan) | 1:53.21 |

**Men's 200m Individual Medley**
| | | |
|---|---|---|
| Gold | Michael Phelps (USA) | 1:54.27 |
| Silver | Ryan Lochte (USA) | 1:54.90 |
| Bronze | Laszlo Cseh (Hungary) | 1:56.22 |

**Men's 400m Individual Medley**
| | | |
|---|---|---|
| Gold | Ryan Lochte (USA) | 4:05.18 |
| Silver | Thiago Pereira (Brazil) | 4:08.86 |
| Bronze | Kosuke Hagino (Japan) | 4:08.94 |

**Men's 4 x 100m Freestyle Relay**
| | | |
|---|---|---|
| Gold | France | 3:09.93 |
| | (Amaury Leveaux, Fabien Gilot, Clement Lefert, Yannick Agnel) | |
| Silver | United States | 3:10.38 |
| Bronze | Russian Fed | 3:11.41 |

**Men's 4 x 200m Freestyle Relay**
| | | |
|---|---|---|
| Gold | United States | 6:59.70 |
| | (Ryan Lochte, Conor Dwyer, Ricky Beren, Michael Phelps) | |
| Silver | France | 7:02.77 |
| Bronze | China | 7:06.30 |

**Men's 4 x 100m Medley Relay**
| | | |
|---|---|---|
| Gold | United States | 3:29.35 |
| | (Matt Grevers, Brendan Hansen, Michael Phelps, Nathan Adrian) | |
| Silver | Japan | 3:31.26 |
| Bronze | Australia | 3:31.58 |

**Men's 10km Marathon Swim**
| | | |
|---|---|---|
| Gold | Oussama Mellouli (Tunisia) | 1:49:55.1 |
| Silver | Thomas Lurz (Germany) | 1:49:58.5 |
| Bronze | Richard Weinberger (Canada) | 1:50:00.3 |

**Women's 50m Freestyle**
| | | |
|---|---|---|
| Gold | Ranomi Kromowidjojo (Netherlands) | 24.05 [OR] |
| Silver | Aliaksandra Herasimenia (Bulgaria) | 24.28 |
| Bronze | Marleen Veldhuis (Netherlands) | 24.39 |

**Women's 100m Freestyle**
| | | |
|---|---|---|
| Gold | Ranomi Kromowidjojo (Netherlands) | 53.00 [OR] |
| Silver | Aliaksandra Herasimenia (Bulgaria) | 53.38 |
| Bronze | Yi Tang (China) | 53.44 |

**Women's 200m Freestyle**
| | | |
|---|---|---|
| Gold | Allison Schmitt (USA) | 1:53.61 [OR] |
| Silver | Camille Muffat (France) | 1:55.58 |
| Bronze | Bronte Barratt (Australia) | 1:55.81 |

**Women's 400m Freestyle**
| | | |
|---|---|---|
| Gold | Camille Muffat (France) | 4:01.45 [OR] |
| Silver | Allison Schmitt (USA) | 4:01.77 |
| Bronze | Rebecca Adlington (GBR) | 4:03.01 |

**Women's 800m Freestyle**
| | | |
|---|---|---|
| Gold | Katie Ledecky (USA) | 8:14.63 |
| Silver | Mireia Garcia (Spain) | 8:18.76 |
| Bronze | Rebecca Adlington (GBR) | 8:20.32 |

# Event results

## Women's 100m Backstroke
Gold  Missy Franklin (USA) .................... 58.33
Silver  Emily Seebohm (Australia) ........... 58.68
Bronze  Aya Terakawa (Japan) .................. 58.83

## Women's 200m Backstroke
Gold  Missy Franklin (USA) .................... 2:04.06 **[WR]**
Silver  Anastasia Zueva (Russian Fed.) 2:05.92
Bronze  Elizabeth Beisel (USA) ................ 2:06.55

## Women's 100m Breaststroke
Gold  Ruta Meilutyte (Lithuania) ............ 1:5.47
Silver  Rebecca Soni (USA) ..................... 1:05.55
Bronze  Satomi Suzuki (Japan) ................. 1:06.46

## Women's 200m Breaststroke
Gold  Rebecca Soni (USA) ..................... 2:19.59 **[WR]**
Silver  Satomi Suzuki (Japan) ................. 2:20.72
Bronze  Iuliia Efimova (Russian Fed.) ....... 2:20.92

## Women's 100m Butterfly
Gold  Dana Vollmer (USA) .................... 55.98 **[WR]**
Silver  Ying Lu (China) ......................... 56.87
Bronze  Alicia Coutts (Australia) ............. 56.94

## Women's 200m Butterfly
Gold  Liuyang Jiao (China) .................... 2:04.06 **[OR]**
Silver  Mireia Garcia (Spain) .................. 2:05.25
Bronze  Natsumi Hoshi (Japan) ............... 2:05.48

## Women's 200m Individual Medley
Gold  Shiwen Ye (China) ...................... 2:7.57 **[OR]**
Silver  Alicia Coutts (Australia) ............. 2:08.15
Bronze  Caitlin Leverenz (USA) ............... 2:08.95

## Women's 400m Individual Medley
Gold  Shiwen Ye (China) ...................... 4:28.43 **[WR]**
Silver  Elizabeth Beisel (USA) ................ 4:31.27
Bronze  Xuanxu Li (China) ..................... 4:32.91

## Women's 4x100m Freestyle Relay
Gold  Australia ................................... 3:33.15 **[OR]**
      (Alicia Coutts, Cate Campbell, Brittany
      Elmsli, Melanie Schlange)
Silver  Netherlands .............................. 3:33.79
Bronze  United States ............................ 3:34.24

## Women's 4 x 200m Freestyle Relay
Gold  United States ............................ 7:42.92 **[OR]**
      (Missy Franklin, Dana Vollmer, Shannon
      Vreelan, Allison Schmitt)
Silver  Australia ................................... 7:44.41
Bronze  France ..................................... 7:47.49

## Women's 4x100m Medley Relay
Gold  United States ............................ 3:52.05 **[WR]**
      (Missy Franklin, Rebecca Soni,
      Dana Vollmer, Allison Schmitt)
Silver  Australia ................................... 3:54.02
Bronze  Japan ...................................... 3:55.73

## Women's 10km Marathon Swim
Gold  Eva Risztov (Hungary) ............... 1:57:38.2
Silver  Haley Anderson (USA) ............... 1:57:38.6
Bronze  Martina Grimaldi (Italy) ............ 1:57:41.8

## Synchronised Swimming
**Duets**
Gold  Russian Federation .................. 197.100
      (Natalia Ishchenko, Svetlana Romashina)
Silver  Spain ....................................... 192.900
      (Ona Carbonell, Andrea Fuentes)
Bronze  China ...................................... 192.870
      (Xuechen Huang, Ou Liu)

**Team**
Gold  Russian Federation .................. 197.030
Silver  China ...................................... 194.010
Bronze  Spain ....................................... 193.120

Women's Singles champion Xiaoxia Li

## Table Tennis
**Men's Singles**
Gold  Jike Zhang (China)
Silver  Hao Wang (China)
Bronze  Dimitrij Ovtcharov (Germany)

**Men's Team**
Gold  China
Silver  Republic of Korea
Bronze  Germany

**Women's Singles**
Gold  Xiaoxia Li (China)
Silver  Ning Ding (China)
Bronze  Tianwei Feng (Singapore)

**Women's Team**
Gold  China
Silver  Japan
Bronze  Singapore

## Taekwondo
**Men's -58kg**
Gold  Joel Gonzalez Bonilla (Spain)
Silver  Daehoon Lee (Republic of Korea)
Bronze  Oscar Munoz Oviedo (Colombia)
Bronze  Alexey Denisenko (Russian Fed.)

**Men's -68kg**
Gold  Servet Tazegul (Turkey)
Silver  Mohammad Bagheri Motamed (Iran)
Bronze  Terrence Jennings (USA)
Bronze  Rohullah Nikpah (Afghanistan)

**Men's -80kg**
Gold  Sebastian Eduardo Crismanich (Argentina)
Silver  Nicolas Garcia Hemme (Spain)
Bronze  Lutalo Muhammad (GBR)
Bronze  Mauro Sarmiento (Italy)

**Men's +80kg**
Gold  Carlo Molfetta (Italy)
Silver  Anthony Obame (Gabon)
Bronze  Robelis Despaigne (Cuba)
Bronze  Xiaobo Liu (China)

**Women's -49kg**
Gold  Jingyu Wu (China)
Silver  Brigitte Yague Enrique (Spain)
Bronze  Lucija Zaninovic (Croatia)
Bronze  Chanatip Sonkham (Thailand)

## Women's -57kg
Gold  Jade Jones (GBR)
Silver  Yuzhuo Hou (China)
Bronze  Marlene Harnois (France)
Bronze  Li-Cheng Tseng (Chinese Taipei)

## Women's -67kg
Gold  Kyung Seon Hwang (Republic of Korea)
Silver  Nur Tatar (Turkey)
Bronze  Paige McPherson (USA)
Bronze  Helena Fromm (Germany)

## Women's +67kg
Gold  Milica Mandic (Serbia)
Silver  Anne-Caroline Graffe (France)
Bronze  Anastasia Baryshnikova (Russian Fed.)
Bronze  Maria Del Rosario Espinoza (Mexico)

## Tennis
**Men's Singles**
Gold  Andy Murray (GBR)
Silver  Roger Federer (Switzerland)
Bronze  Juan Martin Del Potro (Argentina)

**Men's Doubles**
Gold  United States (Mike Bryan, Bob Bryan)
Silver  France (Michael Llodra, Jo-Wilfried Tsonga)
Bronze  France (Julien Benneteau, Richard Gasquet)

**Women's Singles**
Gold  Serena Williams (United States)
Silver  Maria Sharapova (Russian Fed.)
Bronze  Victoria Azarenka (Bulgaria)

**Women's Doubles**
Gold  United States (Serena and Venus Williams)
Silver  Czech Republic (Andrea Hlavackova, Lucie
      Hradecka)
Bronze  Russian Fed. (Maria Kirilenko, Nadia Petrova)

**Mixed Doubles**
Gold  Belarus (Max Mirnyi, Victoria Azarenka)
Silver  Great Britain (Andy Murray, Laura Robson)
Bronze  United States (Mike Bryan, Lisa Raymond)

## Triathlon
**Men**
Gold  Alistair Brownlee (GBR) .............. 1:46:25
Silver  Javier Gomez (Spain) ................. 1:46:36
Bronze  Jonathan Brownlee (GBR) .......... 1:46:56

**Women**
Gold  Nicola Spirig (Switzerland) ....... 1:59.48
Silver  Lisa Norden (Sweden) ................ 1:59:48
Bronze  Erin Densham (Australia) ........... 1:59:50

## Volleyball
**Men**
Gold  Russian Federation
Silver  Brazil
Bronze  Italy

**Women**
Gold  Brazil
Silver  United States
Bronze  Japan

## Water Polo
**Men**
Gold  Croatia
Silver  Italy
Bronze  Serbia

**Women**
| | |
|---|---|
| Gold | United States |
| Silver | Spain |
| Bronze | Australia |

# Weightlifting

**Men's 56kg**
| | | |
|---|---|---|
| Gold | Yun Chol Om *(DPR Korea)* | 293 |
| Silver | Jingbiao Wu *(China)* | 289 |
| Bronze | Valentin Hristov *(Azerbaijan)* | 286 |

**Men's 62kg**
| | | | |
|---|---|---|---|
| Gold | Un Guk Kim *(DPR Korea)* | 327 | **[WR]** |
| Silver | Oscar Mosquera *(Colombia)* | 317 | |
| Bronze | Irawan Eko Yuli *(Indonesia)* | 317 | |

**Men's 69kg**
| | | |
|---|---|---|
| Gold | Qingfeng Lin *(China)* | 344 |
| Silver | Triyatno Triyatno *(Indonesia)* | 333 |
| Bronze | Razvan Martin *(Romania)* | 332 |

**Men's 77kg**
| | | | |
|---|---|---|---|
| Gold | Xiaojun Lu *(China)* | 379 | **[WR]** |
| Silver | Haojie Lu *(China)* | 360 | |
| Bronze | Ivan Rodriguez *(Cuba)* | 349 | |

**Men's 85kg**
| | | |
|---|---|---|
| Gold | Adrian Zielinski *(Poland)* | 385 |
| Silver | Apti Aukhadov *(Russian Fed.)* | 385 |
| Bronze | Kianoush Rostami *(Iran)* | 380 |

**Men's 94kg**
| | | | |
|---|---|---|---|
| Gold | Ilya Ilyin *(Kazakhstan)* | 418 | **[WR]** |
| Silver | Alexandr Ivanov *(Russian Fed.)* | 409 | |
| Bronze | Anatoli Ciricu *(Moldova)* | 407 | |

**Men's 105kg**
| | | |
|---|---|---|
| Gold | Oleksiy Torokhtiy *(Ukraine)* | 412 |
| Silver | Navab Nasirshelal *(Iran)* | 411 |
| Bronze | Bartlomiej Bonk *(Poland)* | 410 |

**Men's +105kg**
| | | |
|---|---|---|
| Gold | Behdad Salimikordasiabi *(Iran)* | 455 |
| Silver | Sajjad Hamlabad *(Iran)* | 449 |
| Bronze | Ruslan Albegov *(Russian Fed.)* | 448 |

**Women's 48kg**
| | | |
|---|---|---|
| Gold | Mingjuan Wang *(China)* | 205 |
| Silver | Hiromi Miyake *(Japan)* | 197 |
| Bronze | Chun Hwa Ryang *(DPR Korea)* | 192 |

**Women's 53kg**
| | | |
|---|---|---|
| Gold | Zulfiya Chinshanlo *(Kazakhstan)* | 226 |
| Silver | Shu-ching Hsu *(Taipei)* | 219 |
| Bronze | Cristina Iovu *(Moldova)* | 219 |

**Women's 58kg**
| | | | |
|---|---|---|---|
| Gold | Xueying Li *(China)* | 246 | **[WR]** |
| Silver | Pimsiri Sirikaew *(Thailand)* | 236 | |
| Bronze | Yuliya Kalina *(Ukraine)* | 235 | |

**Women's 63kg**
| | | | |
|---|---|---|---|
| Gold | Maiya Maneza *(Kazakhstan)* | 245 | **[OR]** |
| Silver | Svetlana Tsarukaeva *(Russian Fed.)* | 237 | |
| Bronze | Christine Girard *(Canada)* | 236 | |

**Women's 69kg**
| | | |
|---|---|---|
| Gold | Jong Sim Rim *(DPR Korea)* | 261 |
| Silver | Roxana Cocos *(Romania)* | 256 |
| Bronze | Maryna Shkermankova *(Bulgaria)* | 256 |

**Women's 75kg**
| | | | |
|---|---|---|---|
| Gold | Svetlana Podobedova *(Kazakhstan)* | 291 | **[OR]** |
| Silver | Natalya Zabolotnaya *(Russian Fed.)* | 291 | **[OR]** |
| Bronze | Iryna Kulesha *(Bulgaria)* | 269 | |

**Women's +75kg**
| | | | |
|---|---|---|---|
| Gold | Lulu Zhou *(China)* | 333 | **[WR]** |
| Silver | Tatiana Kashirina *(Russian Fed.)* | 332 | |
| Bronze | Hripsime Khurshudyan *(Armenia)* | 294 | |

# Wrestling

**Men's Greco-Roman 55kg**
| | |
|---|---|
| Gold | Hamid Soryan *(Iran)* |
| Silver | Rovshan Bayramov *(Azerbaijan)* |
| Bronze | Peter Modos *(Hungary)* |
| Bronze | Mingiyan Semenov *(Russian Fed.)* |

**Men's Greco-Roman 60kg**
| | |
|---|---|
| Gold | Omid Haji Noroozi *(Iran)* |
| Silver | Revaz Lashkhi *(Georgia)* |
| Bronze | Zaur Kuramagomedov *(Russian Fed.)* |
| Bronze | Ryutaro Matsumoto *(Japan)* |

**Men's Greco-Roman 66kg**
| | |
|---|---|
| Gold | Hyeonwoo Kim *(Republic of Korea)* |
| Silver | Tamas Lorincz *(Hungary)* |
| Bronze | Manuchar Tskhadaia *(Georgia)* |
| Bronze | Steeve Guenot *(France)* |

**Men's Greco-Roman 74kg**
| | |
|---|---|
| Gold | Roman Vlasov *(Russian Fed.)* |
| Silver | Arsen Julfalakyan *(Armenia)* |
| Bronze | Aleksandr Kazakevic *(Lithuania)* |
| Bronze | Emin Ahmadov *(Azerbaijan)* |

**Men's Greco-Roman 84kg**
| | |
|---|---|
| Gold | Alan Khugaev *(Russian Fed.)* |
| Silver | Karam Ebrahim *(Egypt)* |
| Bronze | Danyal Gajiyev *(Kazakhstan)* |
| Bronze | Damian Janikowski *(Poland)* |

**Men's Greco-Roman 96kg**
| | |
|---|---|
| Gold | Ghasem Rezaei *(Iran)* |
| Silver | Rustam Totrov *(Russian Fed.)* |
| Bronze | Artur Aleksanyan *(Armenia)* |
| Bronze | Jimmy Lidberg *(Sweden)* |

**Men's Greco-Roman 120kg**
| | |
|---|---|
| Gold | Mijain Lopez Nunez *(Cuba)* |
| Silver | Heiki Nabi *(Estonia)* |
| Bronze | Riza Kayaalp *(Turkey)* |
| Bronze | Johan Euren *(Sweden)* |

**Men's Freestyle 55kg**
| | |
|---|---|
| Gold | Dzhamal Otarsultanov *(Russian Fed.)* |
| Silver | Vladimer Khinchegashvili *(Georgia)* |
| Bronze | Kyong Il Yang *(DPR Korea)* |
| Bronze | Shinichi Yumoto *(Japan)* |

**Men's Freestyle 60kg**
| | |
|---|---|
| Gold | Toghrul Asgarov *(Azerbaijan)* |
| Silver | Besik Kudukhov *(Russian Fed.)* |
| Bronze | Coleman Scott *(USA)* |
| Bronze | Yogeshwar Dutt *(India)* |

**Men's Freestyle 66kg**
| | |
|---|---|
| Gold | Tatsuhiro Yonemitsu *(Japan)* |
| Silver | Sushil Kumar *(India)* |
| Bronze | Akzhurek Tanatarov *(Kazakhstan)* |
| Bronze | Livan Lopez Azcuy *(Cuba)* |

**Men's Freestyle 74kg**
| | |
|---|---|
| Gold | Jordan Burroughs *(USA)* |
| Silver | Sadegh Saeed Goudarzi *(Iran)* |
| Bronze | Soslan Tigiev *(Uzbekistan)* |
| Bronze | Denis Tsargush *(Russian Fed.)* |

**Men's Freestyle 84kg**
| | |
|---|---|
| Gold | Sharif Sharifov *(Azerbaijan)* |
| Silver | Jaime Yusept Espinal *(Puerto Rico)* |
| Bronze | Dato Marsagishvili *(Georgia)* |
| Bronze | Ehsan Naser Lashgari *(Iran)* |

**Men's Freestyle 96kg**
| | |
|---|---|
| Gold | Jacob Varner *(USA)* |
| Silver | Valerii Andriitsev *(Ukraine)* |
| Bronze | Khetag Gazyumov *(Azerbaijan)* |
| Bronze | George Gogshelidze *(Georgia)* |

**Men's Freestyle 120kg**
| | |
|---|---|
| Gold | Artur Taymazov *(Uzbekistan)* |
| Silver | Davit Modzmanashvili *(Georgia)* |
| Bronze | Komeil Ghasemi *(Iran)* |
| Bronze | Bilyal Makhov *(Russian Fed.)* |

**Women's Freestyle 48kg**
| | |
|---|---|
| Gold | Hitomi Obara *(Japan)* |
| Silver | Mariya Stadnyk *(Azerbaijan)* |
| Bronze | Carol Huynh *(Canada)* |
| Bronze | Clarissa Chun *(USA)* |

**Women's Freestyle 55kg**
| | |
|---|---|
| Gold | Saori Yoshida *(Japan)* |
| Silver | Tonya Lynn Verbeek *(Canada)* |
| Bronze | Jackeline Renteria *(Colombia)* |
| Bronze | Yuliya Ratkevich *(Azerbaijan)* |

**Women's Freestyle 63kg**
| | |
|---|---|
| Gold | Kaori Icho *(Japan)* |
| Silver | Ruixue Jing *(China)* |
| Bronze | Battsetseg Soronzonbold *(Mongolia)* |
| Bronze | Lubov Volosova *(Russian Fed.)* |

**Women's Freestyle 72kg**
| | |
|---|---|
| Gold | Natalia Vorobieva *(Russian Fed.)* |
| Silver | Stanka Zlateva Hristova *(Bulgaria)* |
| Bronze | Guzel Manyurova *(Kazakhstan)* |
| Bronze | Maider Unda *(Spain)* |

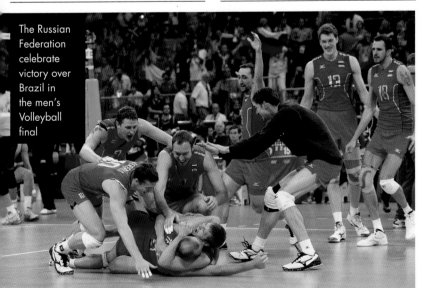

The Russian Federation celebrate victory over Brazil in the men's Volleyball final

*These were happy and glorious Games...
The legacy of the Games of the XXX Olympiad
will become clear in many ways. The human
legacy will reach every region of the world.
Many young people will be inspired to take up
a sport or to pursue their dreams*

*IOC President Jacques Rogge*

Cover Design: Darren Jordan
Design Direction: Darren Jordan
Production: Maria Petalidou
Project Editor: Matthew Lowing

**Picture credits**

All images copyright Press Association Images

**Acknowledgements**

Press Association Sport is a division of The Press Association, the national
news agency of the UK and Ireland, which was founded in 1868.

Head of Content: Peter Marshall
Design: Mark Tattersall
Editor: Andrew McDermott
Contributors: Jack Davies, Frank Malley, Jon Mattos, Peter Thompson

**Below:** Fireworks light up the night
sky over the Olympic Stadium and
the Orbit during the Closing Ceremony
of the London 2012 Olympics Games